John McDonnell

**The Ulster Civil War of 1641 And It's Consequences**

With the History of the Irish Brigade under Montrose in 1644-46

John McDonnell

**The Ulster Civil War of 1641 And It's Consequences**
*With the History of the Irish Brigade under Montrose in 1644-46*

ISBN/EAN: 9783744689762

Printed in Europe, USA, Canada, Australia, Japan

Cover: Foto ©ninafisch / pixelio.de

More available books at **www.hansebooks.com**

# THE ULSTER CIVIL WAR OF 1641,

AND

## ITS CONSEQUENCES

WITH

THE HISTORY OF THE IRISH BRIGADE UNDER

MONTROSE IN 1644-46.

BY

JOHN McDONNELL, M.D.

DUBLIN:
M. H. GILL & SON, UPPER SACKVILLE-STREET.
1879

R. D. WEBB AND SON, PRINTERS, DUBLIN.

# ULSTER CIVIL WAR OF 1641, AND ITS CONSEQUENCES.

# CONTENTS.

## I.

Introductory—Critique of Mr. Froude's transcendental principles of international policy, ... ... ... ... 1

## II.

The causes of the Ulster Insurrection of 1641—The manufacture of rebels and traitors in Dublin Castle, by penniless adventurers, with a view to possess themselves of the forfeited estates of the rebels—Manifesto written by James I. in proof, and absolutely devoid of proof, of a projected rebellion by O'Neill of Tyrone and O'Donnell of Tyrconnell—Condition of the contest between Charles I. and the Long Parliament at the time when the Ulster Irish drew the sword—Character of Parsons, one of the two Lords Justices at this time—Demonstration of the absolute falsehood of the statements of atrocities perpetrated by the Ulster rebels, in a document presented to the Long Parliament by the Irish Government, and in a letter to King Charles from Sir John Temple—Account of the first Massacres in the County of Antrim, ... 6

## III.

Narrative of the campaign of the Montrose Irish Brigade—Their six victories, in three of which, in the battles of Tippermuir, Aberdeen, and Auldern, they constituted fully two-thirds of Montrose's force—In the battles of Inverlochy and Alford they formed about half of the Royalist force; and in the battle of Kilsyth alone they were greatly out-numbered by the Highlanders—Montrose's raid through Breadalbane, Glenorchy, Cantyre, and Lorne, the territories of Argyle, in mid-winter, ... ... ... ... .. ... 70

## IV.

The disastrous defeat of Montrose at Philiphaugh, and defeat in Cantyre, and expulsion from Scotland of Sir Alexander McDonnell—His death in 1647, ... ... ... 114

## V.

Continuation of the War in Ulster—Complete suppression of the rebels by the Protestants of the Plantation—Some account of the government established by the Confederate Catholics of Ireland, ... ... ... ... ... ... 126

## VI.

Events leading to the total ruin of the Irish—Siege of Clonmel by Cromwell, ... ... ... ... ... 151

## VII.

Further proof of extreme exaggeration in the received histories of the war, ... ... ... ... ... ... 155

## VIII.

Account of the proceedings of the rebels in the County Cavan during the first seven months of the war, by the Rev. Mr. Clogy, ... ... ... ... ... ... 161

## IX.

Conclusion—Including some wholesome counsel to both Celt and Saxon, ... ... ... ... ... ... 178

---

## ERRATA.

Page 23, line 21, for "der" *read* "under."
" 74, " 11, for "south-westerly" *read* "south-easterly."
" 79, " 19, for "national" *read* "natural."

### This Sketch

IN VINDICATION OF THE CALUMNIATED ULSTER IRISH IN THE WAR OF

#### 1641

### Is Dedicated to the Memory

OF

## MAJOR-GENERAL SIR ALEXANDER McDONNELL

KNIGHT OF THE FIELD

AND

HIS HEROIC FELLOW-SOLDIERS OF THE MONTROSE IRISH BRIGADE.

# THE ULSTER CIVIL WAR OF 1641 AND ITS CONSEQUENCES.

## I.

I PROPOSE in the following pages to review some of the principal incidents of a period, perhaps the saddest in the sad history of Ireland, including about the last eight years of the reign of Queen Elizabeth—the reigns of James the First of England, and of Charles the First—and five or six years of the reign of the Sword, commonly, but surely facetiously, called the Commonwealth.

The history of Ireland, and of this period especially, has usually been written in the light of the orange or green ray: I am earnestly desirous of writing in the pure white light of truth, which, the scientific reader will recollect, contains both the orange and green, each in its due proportion; but, writing in this spirit, I am well aware that I shall often deeply offend both the factions who have persistently travestied and deformed the history of Ireland from 1172 to 1878. Both parties must admit my facts. To enable them to make what deductions they can with truth from my inferences from my facts, I will furnish them with a few particulars of my biography.

I have been from my early youth to my eighty-third year, steadfastly, "a base, bloody, and brutal Whig," who never failed to promote by his tongue, his pen, and the exercise of his franchise, to the utmost of his little ability, the cause of equal justice to his Roman Catholic fellow-countrymen, from the day (and indeed long before it) on which, according to Lord Clarendon's witty anticipation, as he assumed, the Iron Duke would address the Lords, in his closing speech on Catholic Emancipation, thus:—"My Lords, attention! right about face—quick march"—to the day when the last remnant of political and religious wrong was removed by the crowning and great healing Act for the disestablishment and disendowment of the Established Church of Ireland. I doubt whether any Roman Catholic has more sincerely rejoiced over each step towards this consummation than I have. I may add that I am an uncompromising Protestant, and that it is, in my opinion, clearly the true interest of Ireland to form a part of the British Empire, by an equal, firm, and affectionate union with England and Scotland.

I have entertained the wish for some years past to write an essay on the so-called massacre of 1641 in Ulster, because I thought I had found some overlooked facts relating to it, calculated to throw some of what M. Lanfrey calls "*La lumiére vengeresse de l'histoire*" on the gross and cruel exaggerations of the received accounts of the Ulster insurrection; but I should probably not have taken up my pen, at my years, but for the spur applied by Mr. Froude's *English in Ireland*—a most mischievous production, which is solely calculated to exasperate the Irish by the calumnious virulence of its anti-Irish spirit, and to persuade Englishmen and Scotchmen that the oppression which the Celtic Irish savages had suffered was only too mild for their deserts.

I shall have occasion to refer to this work more than once again; but I wish, *in limine*, to give my opinion here, that Mr. Froude, in the first section of the preliminary chapter of his three volumes, propounds two principles which entirely disentitle him to the office, which I am sure he considers he most worthily fills, of teacher of political morality. He says (vol. i., p. 2):—

"In a world in which we are made to depend so largely for our well-being on the conduct of our neighbours, and yet are created infinitely unequal in ability and worthiness of character, the superior part has a natural right to govern, the inferior part has a natural right to be governed; and a rude but adequate test of superiority and inferiority is provided in the relative strength of the different orders of human beings." Again: "There neither is nor can be an inherent privilege in any person or set of persons to live unworthily at their own will, when they can be led or driven into more honourable courses; the rights of man—if such rights there be—are not to liberty but to wise direction and control."

A more pernicious doctrine than one of these maintains, or a baser than the other, I cannot conceive. In accordance with the former, war would be at once

1*

lighted up from one end of the earth to the other; and the latter would extinguish all patriotic love of country, and all love of liberty. In Europe, it would be the right of Russia to seize upon Sweden and Norway—of the German Empire, upon Denmark—of France, upon Belgium and the Netherlands—of Spain, upon Portugal—and England must surely exercise the right of taking possession of Crete, Cyprus, and Egypt. Italy, for the present, would have to be satisfied with the little republic of San Marino; and Mr. Froude, I presume, would not grudge to Turkey the re-conquest of Greece.

The second principle has certainly this recommendation, that the acceptance of it would keep the peace; but it would be at the sacrifice of some of the noblest virtues that have adorned and immortalized the true heroes of our race. What multitudes of the generous youth of the civilized world have had, and in all future time will have, the flame of love of country and liberty lighted up in their hearts, by the brief and glorious story of Leonidas and his heroic companions. As they read, and their hearts warm as they read, they will assist in imagination at that most touching incident—the celebration by the heroes of their own funeral rites, in the presence of their wives and mothers, on the eve of their departure from Sparta—and will fancy themselves marching with the little phalanx across Peloponessus to Doric strains—

> "Such as raised
> To height of noblest temper heroes old
> Arming to battle: and, instead of rage,
> Deliberate valour breath'd, firm and unmov'd
> With dread of death to flight or foul retreat."

And now they hear the cheers with which the volunteers from Platæa, Corinth, Thespiæ, Ægina, and Athens greet the arrival of the Spartans, and see the united forces occupy the eastern of the two narrow passes that bound the small plain of Thermopylæ, into which they permit the entrance of the enemy, and on which they slaughter, day by day, numbers far exceeding their own of the Medes and the Persian immortals. Lastly, shuddering at the sight of the hordes of Asia descending behind the Greeks by the betrayed mountain-pass, and after the dismissal of the allies, they fancy they hear the ringing shout with which the remnant of his men respond to Leonidas's exhortation on the last morning of their lives—"Fellow-soldiers, make a hearty meal to nerve your arms for this our last battle to-day, for to-night we sup with Pluto." Finally, before quitting the sacred ground, each, standing by the tumulus that covers their dust, hears himself in imagination addressed by the spirits of the departed heroes in the words of the sublime epitaph of Simonides :—

> "Ω ξειν' αγγειλον Λακεδαιμονιοις ὁτι τηδε
> Κειμεθα τοις κεινων ῥημασι πειθομενοι."

> "Stranger, tell the Lacedemonians
> That we lie here in obedience to their precepts."

The incredibly base principle of Froude would have made it the obligation of the Greeks to deliver up Leonidas and Miltiades to the Persians—of the Swiss to surrender Tell to the Austrians—and of the Scots and Americans of the United States to send Wallace, Bruce, and Washington in chains to England, to receive from the halter the reward due to their absurd patriotism and violation of sound principle.

But we need entertain no apprehension that the philosophic nonsense of Mr. Froude, and the wrong-headed Irish faction to which he in truth belongs, will impair the influence which the narratives of this and similar acts of heroic devotion, in past or future time, will ever exercise, to warm the hearts of every generation of the educated youth of the world, and to fill them with patriotic love of country—love of liberty—and detestation of the oppressor.

The principles I have here denounced often crop up in the course of Mr. Froude's history. They form the foundation on which his three volumes are built, and the foundation is rotten.

## II.

The task I have imposed upon myself obliges me, in the first place, to enquire into the grounds of the rebellion of 1641, in Ulster; and to go, for that purpose, so far back as the rebellion of Hugh O'Neill, 3rd Earl of Tyrone, extending over the last eight years of the reign of Elizabeth. This rebellion led indirectly, and an asserted intention to rebel on the part of the same chieftain and O'Donnell of Tyrconnell, in the beginning of the reign of James I., led directly, to the confiscation of six counties in Ulster; and this confiscation, which I undertake to prove to have been an act of perfectly unjustifiable spoliation and outrageous wrong, was a principal, if not the principal cause of the rebellion of 1641.

The suppression of Hugh O'Neill's rebellion was not prosecuted with great vigour for the first five years, although the Queen employed one of her best generals, Sir John Norris, and at one time sent over the unprecedented number of 20,000 men for that purpose.

Norris had attained to great distinction as a soldier in Elizabeth's wars on the Continent, and it is sad to think that any man who achieved good name and fame should have acted the leading part in the following tragedy. In the early part of Norris's career in Ireland, the Earl of Essex was engaged in carving out for himself, with his sword, an estate in Ulster. He was carrying on a desultory war with Sorley Buy (Light-haired Somerled), the leader of the Antrim McDonnells, and had learned that he had sent the women and children, the sick and aged of his clan, to the Island of Rathlin, six or seven miles from the Antrim coast, to be out of reach of Essex's sword. Essex thereupon ordered Norris to take two frigates that were lying off Carrickfergus, troops and artillery, to Rathlin. His orders were, to kill all he could find. On landing, he found Bruce's castle garrisoned by a small body of Sorley Buy's Highlanders, with 200 women and children under their protection, and quickly knocked the outworks of the castle to pieces. (The castle took its name from the circumstance that Robert Bruce had spent a winter in it, in hiding, when his fortunes were at the lowest ebb. It was here he received the lesson from the persevering spider, which induced him to make his final struggle for the crown of Scotland.) The garrison sent to Norris to propose surrender on condition that they should be permitted to return to the Highlands. Norris replied, they must surrender at discretion; and, on their doing so, he first cut their throats, and next those of the 200 women and children. He then proceeded to ferret out from caves round the island and other hiding-places, 400 other victims, whom, to use Mr. Froude's words, "he slaughtered as if they had been seals or otters." Essex sends an account of this terrible tragedy to Elizabeth, whose reply is not the least black incident relating to it.—" I am well pleased with your good service, and will take care to reward John Norris."— That woman's heart must have been made of mill-stone grit.

During the last three years of the war, a frightful change of scene took place under Charles Blount, Lord Mountjoy, Lord Deputy, and afterwards Lord Lieutenant of Ireland and Earl of Devonshire. The war was now carried on on the same principle, if not on the model of the late war in Munster for the destruction of the last Earl of Desmond, the head of the senior branch of the Anglo-Irish Geraldines, the result of which is thus described by the poet Spenser, an eye-witness of what he records :—

" The proof whereof I saw sufficiently exampled in these late wars in Mounster; for notwithstanding that the same was a most rich and plentifull countrey, full of corne and cattle, that you would have thought they should have been able to stand long, yet ere one year and a half they were brought to such wretchednesse, as that any stony heart would have rued the same. Out of every corner of the woods and glynnes, they came creeping forth upon their hands, for their legges could not bear them; they looked like anatomies of death, they spake like ghosts crying out of their graves, they did eat the dead carrions—happy where they could find them, yea, and one another some time after, inasmuch as the very carcases they spared not to scrape out of their graves; and if they found a plot of watercresses or shamrocks, there they flocked as to a feast for the time, yet not able to continue long therewithall; that in short space there were none almost left, and a most populous and plentifull country suddainly left voyde of man and beast; yet sure in all that warre, there perished not many by the sword, but all by the extremities of famine *which they themselves had wrought.*"

Sad contrast to the picture painted by the same poet's pencil as he knew it before the savage war, the responsibility for the consequences of which he so flippantly throws on the victims!

"And sure," says he, "it is a most beautifull and sweet countrey as any is under heaven, being stored throughout with many goodly rivers, replenished with all sorts of fish abundantly, sprinkled with many very sweet islands, and goodley lakes, like little inland seas, that will carry even shippes upon their waters, adorned with goodly woods even fit for building of houses and shippes, so commodiously, as that if some princes in the world had them, they would soone hope to be lords of all the seas, and ere long of all the world: also full of very good ports and havens opening upon England, as inviting us to come to them, to see what excellent commodities the countrey can afford; besides the soyle itself most fertile, fit to yield all kind of fruit that shall be committed thereunto. And lastly, the heavens most milde and temperate, though somewhat more moist than the parts towards the east."

Mr. Froude's vivid picture of this war and its consequences is not less calculated to make the stony heart rue:—

"Every living thing was destroyed by which the insurrection could maintain itself. The corn was burned in the field; the cattle were driven into the camp and slaughtered. The men who could bear arms were out with their chief; the aged and the sick, the women and the little ones perished all in the flames of their burning houses. The official records of this deadly war return the killed and hanged in tens of thousands, and famine took up the work where neither sword nor rope could reach. Finally, when of the proud clan of the southern Geraldines there was none left but a few scattered and desperate bands, the last weapon was produced which never failed to operate. Pardon and reward were offered to those who would kill their comrades, and the bloody heads of noted leaders were brought in sacksful to be paid for in land or money.* The legate, hunted like a wolf, died wretchedly in a forest shanty [hovel]. Desmond himself, after three years of outlaw life, was betrayed by his own people; he was stabbed in his bed, and his head was set on a spike on London-bridge; while so utterly desolate was Munster, that the lowing of a cow, or the sound of a plough-boy's whistle was not to be heard from Valentia to the Rock of Cashel."

Mountjoy carried on in Ulster the same system of warfare, the sword being relentlessly supplemented by fire and famine through three terrible years—the last of Elizabeth's reign, during which, from end to end of Ulster, were continually to be seen and heard the horrid sights and sounds which Coleridge describes as witnessed in his time by the spirits of fire, famine, and slaughter:

"FAMINE ADDRESSING SLAUGHTER.

"Thanks, sister, thanks! the men have bled,
Their wives and their children faint for bread.
I stood in a swampy field of battle,
With bones and skulls I made a rattle,
To frighten the wolf, and carrion crow,
And the homeless dog—but they would not go.
So off I flew: for how could I bear
To see them gorge their dainty fare?
I heard a groan and a peevish squall,
And through the chink of a cottage wall—
Can you guess what I saw there?

---

* I take leave to suggest to Mr. Froude the insertion here, in his next edition, of some little reprobation of this mode of concluding war by subornation of assassination, and the reward of the assassin by pardon and land or money.

" FIRE AND SLAUGHTER.
Whisper it, sister! in our ear.

" FAMINE.
A baby beat its dying mother,
I had starved the one and was starving the other.

. . . .

" FIRE.
Sisters, I from Ireland came!
Hedge and corn-fields all on flame,
I triumphed o'er the setting sun!
And all the time the work was done,
On as I strode with my huge strides,
I flung back my head and held my sides.

. . . .

By the light of his own blazing cot
Was many a naked rebel shot:
The house-stream met the flame and hissed,
While, crash! fell in the roof I wist—
On some of those old bed-rid nurses
That deal in discontent and curses."

" With these chiefs" [Desmond and Tyrone, in the reign of Elizabeth], says Goldwin Smith,* " a long, desperate, and wavering struggle of policy and arms accordingly commenced. It ended in the total overthrow of the chiefs, whose power finally sunk in the fall of Tyrone, but it left Ireland a waste of blood and ashes."

Let us hear the testimony of the chief actor in the tragedy of the Ulster war, and of his private secretary, Fynes Moryson, eye-witnesses of what they describe.

Towards the end of 1602 Tyrone's country had

---

* *Irish History and Irish Character*, p. 72.

been penetrated by Sir Henry Dowcra, a brave and skilful soldier, from Derry in the north; by Sir Arthur Chichester, from Carrickfergus in the east; and by Mountjoy, from the south—till they met in the middle of Tyrone.

"Tyrone" [the Earl], says Mountjoy in a letter to the Council in England, "is already beaten out of his country, and lives in a part of O'Kane's, a place of incredible fastness, where, though it be impossible to do him any great hurt so long as he shall be able to keep any force about him—the ways to him being inaccessible with an army—yet, by lying about him, as we mean to do, we shall in short time put him to his uttermost extremity, and if not light upon his person yet force him to fly the kingdom. In the mean time we can assure your lordships thus much—that from O'Kane's country, where now he liveth, which is to the northward of his own country of Tyrone, we have left none to give us opposition, nor of late have seen any but dead carcasses, merely starved for want of meat, of which kind we found many in divers places as we passed."

On returning to Dublin he directed Dowcra to station himself at Omagh, and Chichester to garrison the fort of Mountjoy, on Lough Neagh, near Dungannon, with orders to drive the inhabitants from Tyrone, to spoil all the corn he could not preserve for the garrison, and to deface all the islands taken.

He writes from Newry, on his way to Dublin, on the 12th of September, that

"In Tyrone, which had been reduced to a desert, and in the neighbouring counties also, he had found everywhere men dead of famine, insomuch that O'Hagan [a chieftain of

Tyrone] protested unto us, that between Tullahogue and Toome [a distance of about twenty miles] there lay a thousand dead, and that since our first drawing this year to Blackwater there were above three thousand starved in Tyrone."

Moryson's testimony is to the same effect :—

"Now because I have often made mention formerly of our destroying the rebels' corn, and using all means to famish them, let me by two or three examples shew the miserable estate to which the rebels were thereby brought. Sir Arthur Chichester, Sir Richard Moryson, and the other commanders of the forces sent against Brian MacArt [O'Neill] aforesaid, in their return homewards saw a most horrid spectacle of three children (whereof the eldest was not above ten years old) all eating their dead mother, upon whose flesh they had fed twenty days past. [I omit here some most revolting particulars.] Former mention hath been made in the Lord Deputy's letters, of carcases scattered in many places—all dead of famine. And no doubt the famine was so great, as the rebel soldiers taking all the common people had to feed upon, and hardly living thereupon (so as they besides fed not only on hawkes, kites, and unsavory birds of prey, but on horse-flesh and other things unfit for man's feeding), as that the common sort were brought to unspeakable extremities (beyond the record of most histories that ever I did read in that kind), the ample relating whereof were an infinite task, yet will I not pass it over without adding some few instances. Captain Trevor and many honest gentlemen lying in the Newry can witness that some old women in those parts were used to make a fire in the fields, and divers little children driving out the cattle in the cold mornings, and coming thither to warm them, were by them surprised, killed, and eaten, which at last was discovered by a great girl breaking from them by the strength of her body; and Captain Trevor sending out soldiers to know the truth, they found the childrens' skulls and bones, and apprehended the old women, who were executed for the fact. The captains of Carrickfergus and the adjacent garrisons of the northern parts can witness that upon the making of peace and receiving the rebels to mercy, it was a common practice among the common sort of them (I mean such as were not sword-men) to thrust long needles into the horses of our English troops, and they dying thereupon, to be ready to tear out one another's throat, for a share of them. And no spectacle was more common in the ditches of towns, and especially in the wasted countries, than to see multitudes of these poor people dead, with their mouths all coloured green by eating nettles, docks, and all things they could rend up above ground. These and very many like lamentable effects followed their rebellion, and no doubt the rebels had been utterly destroyed by famine had not a general peace shortly followed Tyrone's submission."

Soon after Mountjoy's departure to Dublin, Tyrone fled to the mountain fastnesses south-west of Lough Erne in Fermanagh. The utmost force he could now raise was 600 gallowglasses (heavy armed foot) and kerne (light armed foot), and fifty horse. Nearly all his vassals and allies, O'Donnell and O'Kane amongst them, had made their peace, and he himself, reduced to despair, repeatedly made the most urgent appeals to Mountjoy for mercy and solemn promises of the most submissive loyalty to Elizabeth for the rest of his life. He wrote upon 12th November, 1602 :—

"I will, from henceforth," says he, "both renounce all other princes but her, and serve her highness the residue of my life, humbly requesting of your honor, now that you have brought me so low, to remember I am a nobleman, and to take compassion on me, that the overthrow of my house and posterity may be prevented by your good means and honorable care towards her Majesty for me, which with all humility I desire and will accept."

Early in 1603, when Elizabeth was on her deathbed, Mountjoy permitted O'Neill to appear before him at Mellifont, near Drogheda, and there the proud but humiliated chieftain, on his knees before the Lord Deputy for an hour, made ample confession of the wickedness of his rebellion, and renewed protestations of future loyalty, and received pardon.

I have entered thus particularly into the history of this rebellion, because it affords a demonstration that O'Neill and O'Donnell could not have entertained the thought of a new rebellion within four years of O'Neill's submission, or before the half-starved Ulster youth of 1603 had ripened into fighting men. Under the circumstances, no man, not a cross between a lunatic and an idiot, could have entertained the thought for a moment.

One of the worst evils that afflicted Ireland for centuries arose from a succession of penniless adventurers who flocked to Dublin Castle, and by virtue of a manufacture, at this time brought to great perfection, became, in short space, lords of broad and fertile lands. It may with perfect confidence be asserted, that if the manufactures of iron, flax, silk, wool, and cotton-wool had been brought here to the same condition of perfection, Ireland would long have been, instead of the poorest and most manufactureless country in Europe, the most rife of manufacture and the richest of all countries. I allude to the manufacture in Dublin Castle of Irish traitors and rebels, whose confiscated lands the adventurers were resolved to be possessed of. Goldwin Smith, speaking of the spirit of adventure so prevalent in the time of Elizabeth, says :—

"The eagles took wing for the Spanish main; the vultures descended upon Ireland. A daring use of his sword procured for the adventurer in the Spanish colonies romantic wealth in the shape of ingots and rich bales; a dexterous use of intrigue, chicanery, and the art of inciting to rebellion, procured for the sharper in Ireland wealth less romantic, but more solid and lasting, in the shape of confiscated lands. The appearance of these adventurers, and the commencement of their hateful trade, made war internecine. Submission may avail with the tyrant, but never with the confiscator."

The raw material, in the present instance, was most unpromising, but the operatives were not discouraged, and their audacity was approved by perfect success. The process of manufacture was very simple. An anonymous letter, addressed to Sir William Usher, Clerk of the Privy Council, was dropt in the Council chamber, stating that O'Neill, O'Donnell, and Richard Nugent, a young man, Baron of Delvin, had entered into a conspiracy to seize the Castle of Dublin, put the Lord-Deputy to death, and raise a general rebellion with the aid of a Spanish army. "Experience," says the proverb, "keeps a dear school, but fools will learn at no other." The chieftains had a terrible lesson from that teacher four years before. They knew that Elizabeth had sent 20,000 men to subdue them, and that she had utterly crushed them with half that number—that the resources of James were the same with the addition of those of Scotland; and that at this time by no possibility could they bring 2,000 men into the field. They knew, too, that their lives would assuredly be forfeited if they submitted themselves to the government for trial.

Delvin was taken into custody, tried, and condemned, but effected his escape.

O'Neill and O'Donnell, with their families, immediately fled from Ireland, and ended their days in Rome. Two, and two only, plausible facts have ever been urged against them in proof of their guilt, viz.: (1) their flight, and (2) that they never published any vindication of themselves at Rome.

The answer to the former charge is very simple. If either of them had been asked why he did not stand his trial, "he might have answered as another unfortunate Irish exile did in a similar case :—' What chance would a fat goose have before a jury of foxes?' "*

No satisfactory answer has been given, so far as I know, to the argument that they never published any vindication of themselves; yet I think this fact admits of an explanation both satisfactory and obvious. They

* Cooke Taylor's *Civil Wars of Ireland.*

depended in Rome for the support of themselves and their families altogether upon the pensions liberally bestowed upon them by Philip of Spain and the Pope, for the very reason that they were believed to have been ever irreconcilable enemies of England; and nothing can be more certain than that the publication by them of a statement clearly proving that, at the time of their flight, they were devotedly loyal to James, and neither did nor could have contemplated the raising an Irish rebellion against him, would at once have deprived them of their sole means of subsistence.

James soon published a manifesto from his own pen to justify before the world the attainder about to be passed against the fugitives, and to make their guilt manifest. This document contains much extremely undignified vituperation of them, but not a shadow of proof of their guilt. It may fairly be supposed to contain all the evidence he was able to produce. I give the manifesto *in extenso* that the reader may judge of it for himself.

"BY THE KING: A PROCLAMATION TOUCHING THE EARLS OF TIRONE AND TIRCONNEL.

"Seeing it is common and natural in all persons of what condition soever, to speak and judge variably of all new and sudden accidents, and that the flight of the Earles of Tirone and Tirconnel, with some others of their followers out of the north parts of our realm of Ireland, may haply prove a subject of like discourse: We have thought it not amiss to deliver some such matter in publique, as may better cleare men's judgements concerning the same; not in respect of any worth or value in these men's persons, being base and rude in their originall, but to take away all such inconveniences as may blemish the reputation of that friendship, which ought to be mutually observed between us and other princes. For although it is not unlikely that the report of their titles and dignities may draw from princes and states some such courtesies at their first coming abroad, as are incident to men of extraordinary rank and qualitie, yet, when wee have taken the best means wee can to lay them open in every condition, wee shall then expect from our friends and neighbours all such just and noble proceedings as stand with the rules of honour and friendship, and from our subjects, at home and abroad, that duety and obedience (in their carriage towards them) which they owe to us by inseparable bonds and obligations of nature and loyaltie, whereof wee intend to take streight accompt. For which purpose wee do hereby first declare, that these persons above-mentioned had not their creations or possessions in regard of any lineall or lawfull descent from ancestors of blood or vertue; but were onely preferred by the late Queene our sister, of famous memorie, and by ourselves, for some reasons of state, before others who for their qualitie and birth (in those provinces where they dwell) might better have challenged those honours which were conferred upon them. Secondly, wee doe professe that it is knowen to our counsell here, and to our deputie and state there, and so shall it appeare to the world (as cleare as the sunne) by evident proofes, the onely ground and motive of this high contempt in these men's departure, hath been the private knowledge and inward terror of their owne guiltinesse: whereof, because wee heare that they doe seeke to take away the blot and infamie, by divulging that they have withdrawn themselves for matters of religion (a cloake that serves too much in these days to cover many evil intentions) adding also thereunto some other vaine pretexts of receiving injustice, when their rights and claims have come in question between them and us, or any of our subjects and them, wee think not impertinent to say somewhat thereof.

"And therefore, although wee judge it needlesse to seeke for many arguments to confirme whatsoever shall be said of these men's corruption and falshood (whose heinous offences remaine so fresh in memorie, since they declared themselves so very monsters in nature, as they did not onely withdraw from their personal obedience to their soverigne, but were content to sell over their native countrey to those that stood at that time in the highest terms of hostilitie with the two crowns of England and Ireland) yet, to make the absurditie and ingratitude of the allegations abovementioned, so much the more cleare to all men of equall judgement, wee doe hereby professe on the word of a kinge that there never was as much as any shadowe of molestation, nor purpose of proceeding in any degree against them for matter concerning religion. Such being their condition and profession, to think murder no fault, marriage of no use, nor any man worthy to be esteemed valiant that did not glorie in rapine and opression; as wee should have thought an unreasonable thing to trouble them for any different point in religion, before any man could perceive by their conversation that they made truely conscience of any religion. So doe wee also for the second part of their excuse affirm, that (notwithstanding all that they can claime must be acknowledged to proceed from mere grace upon their submission, after their great and unnaturale treasons) there hath never come any question concerning their rights or possessions wherein wee have not bene inclinable to showe them favour than to any of their competitours, except in those cases wherein wee have plainly discerned that their onely end was to have made themselves more able than now they are to resist all lawfull authoritie (when they should returne to their vomit again) by usurping a power over other good subjects of ours that dwell among them, better borne than they, and utterly disclaiming from any dependancie upon them.

"Having now delivered this much concerning these men's estates and their proceedings, wee will onely end with this conclusion, that they shall not be able to denie, whensoever they should dare to present themselves before the seate of justice, that they have (before the running out of our kingdom) not onely entered into combination for stirring sedition and intestine rebellion, but have directed divers instruments, as well priestes as others, to make offers to foreign states and princes (if they had bene as ready to receive them) of their readinesse and resolution to adhere to them whensoever they should seeke to invade that kingdom. Wherein, amongst other things, this is not to be forgotten, that under condition of being made free from English government, they resolved also to comprehend the utter extirpation of all those subjects that are now remayning alive within that kingdom, formerly descended from the English race. In which practices and propositions, followed and fomented by priestes and jesuites (of whose function in these times the practice and persuasion of subjects to rebel against their soveraignes is one special and essential part and portion) as they have found no such encouragement as they expected and have boasted of, so wee doe assure ourselves, that when this declaration shall bee seene and duely weighed with all due circumstances, it will bee of force sufficient to disperse and to discredit all such untrueths, as these contemptible creatures, so full of infidelity and ingratitude, shall disgorge against us and our just and moderate proceeding, and shall procure unto them no better usage than they would wish should bee afforded to any such packe of rebels, borne their subjects, and bound unto them in so many and so great obligations.

"Given at our palace of Westminster, the fifteenth day of November, in the fifth yeere of our reigne of Great Britain, France, and Ireland. GOD SAVE THE KING."

The world was favoured in this proclamation with much vulgar and false abuse of the Earls, and mere assertion, without proof of any kind of their guilt. But though James fails conspicuously in this respect, he furnished shortly after a singular piece of evidence in favour of their innocence. Baron Delvin, one of the alleged conspirators already mentioned, surrendered himself to James, was soon after in high favour with him, and was created by him Earl of Westmeath. The evidence against O'Neill and O'Donnell, however flimsy, was abundantly sufficient to procure their attainder and the confiscation of their vast estates by Act of Parliament in 1613, to be at the disposal of the King. By a crowning act of incredible injustice, all who held lands under the chiefs, however innocent of complicity, forfeited them. An insane rebellion of Sir Cahir O'Dogherty, soon after, added Innishowen to the other immense forfeitures, and James was enabled to undertake the grateful task of executing the Plantation of Ulster, and the introduction of civility, by such means, into the North of Ireland.

Thus, by an act of atrocious and lawless cruelty, der the mask of law, were six counties of Ulster forfeited to the Crown. The passive submission of the despoiled natives affords strong corroboration of what I have stated as to the nearly complete destruction of the fighting men of the population.

"By this last treason," says Mr. Froude, "of the two Earls and their confederates, six counties were escheated to the Crown—Donegall, Derry, Tyrone, Fermanagh, Cavan, and

Armagh. Antrim and Down were already partially occupied by Scots—western Highlanders, who for three centuries had been forming settlements in Ireland. They had been scarcely distinguishable hitherto from the native race, but they were capable of being reclaimed. Their chief, Sir Randal MacDonnell, or MacConnell, was created Earl of Antrim. The six escheated counties contained in all two million acres. Of these, a million and a-half bog, forest, and mountain were restored to the Irish. The half-million were settled with families of Scotch and English Protestants."

This passage affords a specimen of Mr. Froude's historical research and accuracy. About 250 years before the Plantation of Ulster, Ian Vohr McDonnell, of Isla and Cantyre, second son of the Lord of the Isles, married Margery Byssett, heiress of a Norman Baron, lord of the district of the Glens in the County of Antrim. At the time of the confiscation, Ian Vohr's descendants possessed the county from Larne to Dunluce. In Antrim, south of Larne, and in Down, there were no western Highlanders, who, though "capable of being reclaimed," were not "alien" to the Irish either "in blood, language, or religion," except the Campbells, who were aliens in religion. The Western Highlanders were more purely Celtic than the Irish themselves. The Celtic blood of Ireland had received a considerable infusion of Norman and Saxon blood between 1172 and 1600. Up to this time, and indeed till the Highland chiefs discovered that their importance had come to depend more on the number of their sheep than of their clansmen, the Western Highlanders had repelled the Sassenach. The O'Neills still held large estates in the south of Antrim, and in the County Down; and Lord Montgomery of Ards, and Lord Clandeboy (Hamilton), both from Ayrshire, had lately acquired, by less questionable means than usual, extensive properties in Down. The Savages who had accompanied DeCourcy in his raid at the time of the English invasion, still possessed the Ards of Down; and, in the south of the county, the Magennisses and FitzGeralds were considerable landed proprietors.

"Two million acres," says Mr. Froude, "were confiscated." Donegal and Tyrone alone contain 1,999,736 acres. We must surely admire the singular generosity with which three-fourths of the forfeited lands were assigned to the natives. It was, however, a drawback that they were "bog, forest, and mountain." The king-craft by which this cruel spoliation was perpetrated had not attained its present perfection, through the skill of an inexperienced craftsman. James had, shortly before, "tried his prentice hand" in spoliation and worse, in the Highlands of Scotland. Sir James McDonnell (chief of the Randal McDonnell just mentioned), whose Highland designation was McDonnell of Isla, Cantyre, and the Glens, and whose family, though not the main branch of the clan MacDonald, had been for more than a century past the most powerful one of that clan, had been engaged for some years in rebellious war with James, zealously assisted by the Argyle Campbells. Desirous of strengthening himself against the rebel, he entered into a negotiation with the Marquis of Huntly, chief of the powerful clan Gordon, to aid in the destruction of McDonnell.

"In a short time," says Gregory in his *History of the Western Highlands and Isles of Scotland* (p. 313, *et seq.*), "the King's pleasure was signified to the Council that certain conditions, sent direct from the Court, should be proposed for the Marquis's [Huntly's] acceptance. It is scarcely credible that such conditions should have emanated from a King of Great Britain in the 17th century; yet there seems no reason to doubt that, if not originally suggested by James himself, they certainly received his approval."

They were as follows :—

"That the Marquis should undertake the service upon his own private means alone; that he should conclude it within a year; that he should end the service, not by agreement with the country people, but by exterminating them."

By a mere accident the undertaking of the massacre was prevented. Gregory adds :—

"This accident, for it does not bear the appearance of a scheme concerted to save the Islanders, seems alone to have prevented the reign of James VI. from being stained by a massacre which, for atrocity and the deliberation with which it was planned, would have left that of Glenco far in the shade. But whether the interference of the Presbyterians was accidental or intentional, the islanders of that day owed nothing to their prince, whose character must ever bear the stain of having, for the most sordid motives, consigned to destruction thousands of his subjects."

The second great cause of the insurrection of 1641 was the religious persecution of the Irish Roman Catholics during the whole of our period, and the political tyranny they suffered under during the reigns of James, Charles, and the Sword. Early in the reign of Elizabeth, she resolved to establish the Reformation in Ireland, and, with that view, a fine of twelve pence each Sunday was to be imposed upon all who refused to attend divine worship in the Protestant churches; and, so far as the power of her bayonets reached, the property of the Romish Church was bestowed upon that of the Reformation, and the Irish bishops and inferior clergy were displaced by imported Englishmen. At this time probably not one person in fifty, beyond the walls of Dublin, could speak English, and of course the imported clergy could not speak Irish. I fancy there are few Protestants at the present time who would dispute my opinion, that if Satan himself had presided at the council where the adoption of these measures was resolved upon, they were precisely those he would have suggested and advocated with the certainty of rendering Protestants hateful in the eyes of the Irish and the Reformation among them impossible.

I beg leave to put the following case and question before any English or Scotch Protestant. If, in the reigns of Elizabeth and James VI., a malignant fate had put it in the power of the Roman Catholic minority in England and Scotland, with the aid of French and Spanish bayonets, to have established in them the Roman Catholic religion, to have bestowed the property of the established churches upon Roman Catholic bishops and priests, speaking Irish or Italian, what would have been the speedy consequence? Assuredly there would have been formed an immediate "solemn league and covenant," from John O'Groat's to St. Michael's Mount, and an insurrection, which for a few months would have been called a rebellion, but soon, on its certain success, a civil war for the redress of intolerable tyranny and wrong. Let the person to whom I have put the above query recollect that a precisely similar wrong was only one of several that provoked the rebellion of 1641 in Ulster.

For some time before his death, James was zealously engaged in a project to repeat in Connaught the public robbery he had so successfully perpetrated in Ulster. He proposed to establish an inquisition into the legality of the titles of the landed gentry of Connaught to property possessed by them for centuries. In the event of any flaw in the title being discovered by a keen lawyer's eye, the land was to be forfeited to the Crown. The iniquity of this project was aggravated by what had already occurred respecting these lands. In the reign of Elizabeth, the lords and gentry of Connaught had surrendered their estates to the Lord Deputy, Sir John Perrot, receiving them back as grants from the Queen.

They neglected to enrol their patents, and surrendered them to James, paying £3,000 to have them enrolled. The officers of the Court of Chancery negligently, if not fraudulently, omitted this form, and James, at the time of his death, was preparing to avail himself of this clerical omission, and debating with himself whether he would carry out the confiscation, or accept a bribe of £10,000 offered him by the gentry to secure themselves against his rapacity. Thus ended, so far as Ireland was concerned, the disgraceful reign of the first of five sovereigns of his race, every one of whom oppressed and inflicted cruel and insufferable wrongs upon the unfortunate country cursed with their misrule.

The scheme of confiscation thus came to Charles as an inheritance from his father. The lords and gentry of Connaught now submitted to Charles a series of propositions, a sort of "Bill of Rights," for the pacification of the country, and the securing of their properties. These propositions were called the graces. They were founded both in equity and sound policy. There was not one of them which a wise and good king would not have granted willingly, without hesitation, and without bribe. The most important articles of them were : —

"That whereby the subjects were secured in the quiet enjoyment of their lands, by limiting the King's title to sixty years (and renouncing all claims of any earlier period); that which admitted the recusants to sue their liveries, ouster-le-mains, and other grants, depending in the court of wards, and to practise in the law courts, on taking an oath substituted in the place of the oath of supremacy, by which they professed to acknowledge and promised to defend Charles as the rightful and lawful King of the realm; and that which admitted the inhabitants of Connaught to make a new enrolment of their patents, and thus to secure their titles from future litigation." (Leland, vol. ii., p. 498, Cork, 1775.)

The oppressions of the soldiery were to be restrained, martial law was to be confined to times of war and rebellion, persons notoriously infamous or capitally convicted were not to be permitted to be witnesses, and the clergy were not to keep private prisons for persons accused of ecclesiastical offences.

Charles was, however, offered the bribe of £120,000, and was guilty, after accepting the bribe, of the scarcely credible baseness and breach of faith, of first evading, and finally permitting and encouraging the Lord Deputy Wentworth to refuse the graces. The tyranny exercised in his government of Ireland, by "that great bad man,"* was a most powerful immediate cause of the outbreak of 1641. Whoever, with a little skill in physiognomy, has looked upon him as presented to us in Van Dyke's living portrait, and has marked the stern countenance, falcon eye, gauntleted and truncheoned hand and arm standing out of the canvas, will feel that he must have been by nature a tyrant. Nothing could exceed the insolence and contempt of justice with which, by a mixture of legal chicane, bribery of the judges, and intimidation of the juries,

* Epithets bestowed by Burke upon another tyrant, Cromwell.

he proceeded to effect his iniquitous project. In attending the legal process in each county, he took with him " 500 horse, as good lookers-on." He gave the judges a share (4s. in the pound out of the first year's rent to the Chief Justice and Chief Baron) of the plunder in each case decided in favour of the Crown; and in the first case in which a jury in the County of Galway (in which county only he met with opposition) found for the proprietors, he fined the sheriff £1,000 for returning an improper jury, and summoned the jury to appear before the Castle Chamber (the Irish Star Chamber), by which they were fined £4,000 each, and to be imprisoned till the fines were paid, and till they had confessed their offence before the court on their knees. He enforced, individually, against the Roman Catholic lawyers, who had pleaded against the title of the Crown in the Galway trials, the law which required their taking the oath of supremacy; their refusing to take which disqualified them for the exercise of their profession, and their taking of which amounted to the renouncing of their religion.* By an extortion, which he had afterwards good reason to rue, he obliged the London companies to pay £70,000 for neglect of certain of the conditions of the grant by James of their estates in the County of Londonderry. He considered Ireland as a con-

* Cooke Taylor, vol. i., p. 254; and Wright's *History of Ireland*, vol. i., p. 641.

quered country, which, consequently, in his opinion, possessed no civil rights, except such as it should please Charles to grant. These sentiments he avowed and defended at the trial where he was condemned to death. The whole of his government, during the years of his rule as Lord Deputy or Lord Lieutenant, was in harmony with them; and in the end he was able proudly to boast, in a letter to Laud—

"Now I can say the King is as absolute here as any prince in the whole world can be, and may be still, if it be not spoiled on that side" [viz., in England]. Wright, *ubi supra*, vol. i., p. 639.

The tyranny exercised by Strafford powerfully contributed to excite the impending Ulster outbreak of 1641. The proposed confiscation in Connaught did not indeed directly affect the Roman Catholics of Ulster; but they had suffered and were suffering under a similar outrage, and therefore the more warmly and deeply sympathised with their brethren in Connaught, and resented the threatened wrong. The penal laws against Roman Catholics, then in existence, though mild indeed in comparison with what that disgraceful and demoralising code became in the reign of Queen Anne, and though both James and Charles were usually desirous of letting them slumber, could be put in force at any time by the Government, as we have just seen in the case of the Roman Catholic lawyers who had pleaded against James's title in the Galway confiscation case, or by any spiteful enemy, in the case of an individual Roman Catholic. Strafford, shortly before this time, coerced the Roman Catholics to submit to a tax he proposed to establish, by the threat that, in the event of their refusal, he would strictly enforce the law which imposed the weekly fine of one shilling upon all who did not attend Divine service in the churches of the Establishment. The public performance of Divine service by the Roman Catholic clergy was usually winked at; but the following occurrence, shortly before Strafford's Lord Deputyship, shows the sort of security afforded by the sufferance in question :—

"The Lords Justices were attending Divine service at Christ Church [a Protestant Cathedral in Dublin], when intelligence reached them that a fraternity of Carmelites were celebrating their religious rites, in the habits of their order, in a part of Dublin called Cook-street. Nothing had given greater offence to the English Protestants than the appearance of the monastic orders, and the behaviour of these friars was looked upon as an act of presumptuous contumacy. The Archbishop of Dublin, with the chief magistrate of the city, proceeded to Cook-street, at the head of a file of musketeers, entered the chapel, seized the priest in his vestments, and carried away all the sacred utensils and ornaments. In the first moments of alarm the congregation sought their safety in flight, but some of them returned, and, pursuing the assailants, they succeeded in rescuing their priest. A strong representation of the conduct of the Catholics on this occasion was sent over to the Privy Council in London, and the more zealous Protestants seized the occasion to protest against what they conceived to be the mistaken lenity which had encouraged such bold displays. It was therefore resolved to punish the religious orders in general; and by the Council's order sixteen monastic houses were seized to the King's use, and the Popish College in Dublin, which from its first establishment had been looked upon with a jealous eye, was granted to the University of Dublin, and converted into a Protestant seminary." [*]

These exasperating and oppressive laws had their share in exciting to insurrection. If enforced, no Roman Catholic could plead as counsel in a court of justice, be a magistrate, or hold any office, civil or military, under the Crown, and wards in Chancery, sons of Roman Catholics, were to be brought up Protestants.

The last motive to the insurrection in 1641 was the desire to support Charles against the Puritan Parliamentarians. The Roman Catholic gentry of Ireland were to a man Cavaliers. They were Royalists by their religion, and knew that Charles was not disposed to oppress them on account of their religion. They knew that the Long Parliament had proclaimed their determination to extirpate that religion in Ireland, which, to people attached devotedly to it as the Irish were, was tantamount to a declaration of a determination to extirpate themselves; and they had good reason to suspect that the intention to perpetrate this atrocious wickedness was really entertained by the stern leaders of the Puritan party in England and Scotland.

At this point of time, when the Irish Roman Catholics

---

[*] Wright's *History of Ireland*, vol. i., p. 264.

resolved to draw the sword in defence of the Royal prerogative, among other motives, it is right to advert to the exact condition at which the quarrel between Charles and his parliament had arrived.

"Neither party," says Macaulay *(History of England,* vol. i., p. 103, *et seq.),* "wanted strong arguments for the measures which it was disposed to adopt. The reasoning of the most enlightened Royalists may be summed up thus: 'It is true that great abuses have existed; but they have been redressed. It is true that precious rights have been invaded; but they have been vindicated and surrounded with new securities. The sittings of the estates of the realm have been, in defiance of all precedent and of the spirit of the constitution, intermitted during eleven years; but it has been provided that henceforth three years shall never elapse without a parliament. The Star Chamber, the High Commission, the Council of York, oppressed and plundered us; but these hateful courts have now ceased to exist. The Lord Lieutenant [Strafford] aimed at establishing military despotism; but he has answered for his treason with his head. The Primate [Archbishop Laud] tainted our worship with Popish rites, and punished our scruples with Popish cruelty; but he is awaiting in the Tower the judgment of his peers. The Lord Keeper sanctioned a plan by which the property of every man in England was placed at the mercy of the Crown; but he has been disgraced, ruined, and compelled to take refuge in a foreign land. The ministers of tyranny have expiated their crimes. The victims of tyranny have been compensated for their sufferings. Under these circumstances it would be unwise to persevere in that course which was justifiable and necessary when we first met, after a long interval, and found the whole administration one mass of abuses. It is time to take heed that we do not so pursue our victory over despotism as to run into anarchy. It was not in our power to overturn the bad institutions which lately afflicted our country, without shocks which have loosened the foundations of government. Now that those institutions have fallen, we must hasten to prop the edifice which it was lately our duty to batter. Henceforth it will be our wisdom to look with jealousy on schemes of innovation, and to guard from encroachment all the prerogatives with which the law has, for the public good, armed the sovereign.' Such were the views of those men of whom the excellent Falkland may be regarded as the leader, 'a beautiful model,' says Lord Woodhouselee, 'of the most exalted and virtuous patriotism.'"

In short, the victory of the Long Parliament over Charles was now complete, by virtue of the use of the constitutional weapon, viz., the right of voting or withholding the supplies, against which he was provided with no defensive armour of more avail than would have been the "tissue of woven air" in which some lady novelist has clothed her heroine, and by the firm and steady use of which every other reform which the nation deliberately desired could be procured. The Celtic Irish were far from having such a weapon against the tyranny of Strafford. They had none.

I am far from undertaking to answer for it, that if Charles had been victorious, he and his Irish Cavaliers would have been satisfied that he should be confirmed simply in his now limited prerogatives; but, at all events, their utter defeat prevented their showing the world how far they would have gone, if victorious. This I think is the sole advantage Charles has had over his enemies. Their success enabled them to demonstrate that their policy was to end in the utter subversion of the Constitution, and the substitution of sword-law under Oliver I. The first great stride towards this consummation had already been taken, by the Act passed (before the ink of a statute establishing triennial parliaments was well dry), depriving the King of the power of dissolving this Parliament without the consent of the two houses. By his consent to this Act, Charles sealed his own fate. He deprived himself of his time-honoured prerogative; but this was of small importance indeed compared with the prerogative of which it deprived the people of England. It was their unquestioned right, at each election of members of the House of Commons, to control and direct the government of the country, by the return of members whose political sentiments accorded with their own. If the Triennial Act had taken root, the first House of Commons elected under it, by a people exasperated by Charles's tyranny, would no doubt have acted just as the Long Parliament at first did; but it is to me perfectly incredible, that they would not, before 1649, have returned an overwhelming majority to stay the impending ruin of the Constitution; and Charles would either have faithfully carried out his solemn and public protestation* before his whole army,

* " I do promise, in the presence of Almighty God, and as I hope for his blessing and protection, that I will to the utmost of my power, defend and maintain the reformed Protestant religion, established in the Church of England, and by the Grace of God in the same will live and die.

" I desire that the laws may ever be the measure of my government, or he would have been dethroned as infamous and faithless, and his crown have been bestowed upon his son; not as it was in 1660, but with well-defined and strictly constitutional limitations; and the nation and the saints would have been spared the crime, or as Tallyrand would have preferred to call it, " worse, the blunder," of the murder of Charles.

I know of no two persons of their time more worthy of profound commiseration than Charles I. and his grandmother. Mary came to Scotland, a widow, still in her teens, to be advised and guided by a band of statesmen as hard-headed and hard-hearted, astute and selfish, as could be found at that time in any court of Christendom. Her government was conducted with surprising good sense and discretion till the sad day of her most unfortunate marriage with Darnley, whom

and that the liberty and property of the subject may be preserved by them with the same care as my own just rights. And if it please God, by his blessing on this army, raised for my necessary defence, to preserve me from the present rebellion, I do solemnly and faithfully promise in the sight of God to maintain the just privileges and freedom of Parliament, and to govern to the utmost of my power by the known statutes and customs of the kingdom, and particularly to observe inviolably the laws to which I have given my consent this parliament. Meanwhile if this emergence, and the great necessity to which I am driven, beget any violation of law, I hope it shall be imputed by God and man to the authors of this war, not to me, who have so earnestly sought to preserve the peace of the kingdom.

" When I willingly fail in these particulars, I shall expect no aid or relief from man, nor any protection from above. But in this resolution I hope for the cheerful assistance of all good men, and am confident of the blessing of Heaven."

The date of this protestation was October, 1642, shortly before the battle of Edge Hill.

I will not call a brainless and heartless brute, because of my regard and respect for my horse and dog (animals morally very superior to him); but assuredly this marriage was at the root of her ruin. It was not possible that she should not rejoice at his death, but I am convinced she was not guilty of it. Her marriage with Bothwell was an act of insanity; but she expiated her errors and sins by a terrible punishment—by her eighteen years' imprisonment, one day of which Elizabeth had not the shadow of a right to inflict. Well might she, as each Spring of her weary bondage returned, lament in the touching words Burns puts into her mouth:—

> "Now blooms the lily on the bank,
> The primrose down the brae,
> The hawthorn's budding in the glen,
> And milk-white is the slae.
> The meanest hind in fair Scotland
> May rove their sweets amang,
> But I the Queen of all Scotland
> Maun bide in prison strang."

Equally unjustifiable was her execution, after Elizabeth had failed in her attempt to suborn the despatch of her cousin-queen in private, by her keeper.

I hold that Charles I. also is worthy of great commiseration. He was a despot, and it was the duty no less than the right of his subjects to demand and secure, if necessary at the sword's point, the reasonable and constitutional liberties which had been, in fact, granted by Charles, and secured by Act of Parliament in 1641. But it should not be forgotten, in mitigation of our condemnation of him, that his father preached to him from his cradle that kings reign by right divine, and that he was misled, too, by the example of his arbitrary predecessors from Henry VII. to 1625; yet he never addressed his loving Commons thus: "I discharge you from presuming to meddle with state affairs, which are matters above your comprehension," as Elizabeth did; nor did he ever pack a House of Commons as James did in Ireland, and defend his creation of forty boroughs for that purpose with characteristic unwisdom by a fool-born jest—

"What is it to you," said James to the gentlemen deputed to remonstrate against the proceeding, "whether I make many or few boroughs? My council may consider the fitness, if I require it. But what if I had made forty noblemen and four hundred boroughs? The more, the merrier; the fewer, the better cheer!"

And if Charles had been permitted to live a few years longer, how he might have marvelled at his own moderation, on hearing that Cromwell had expelled, by Pride's chalybeate purge, about 200 members of the House of Commons, at the point of the bayonet, to ensure his having a mockery of a House of Commons that would cashier the House of Lords, and vote the death of Charles.

I have now put before the reader the three great

causes of the Ulster rebellion of 1641 : First, the cruel and perfectly unjust confiscation of the lands immemorially possessed by the people of six counties of the province. Secondly, the oppression suffered under penal laws by all the Roman Catholics of Ireland, and the grinding tyranny established by Strafford. And thirdly, the strong desire to support their somewhat friendly King against their inveterate and detested enemies, the Puritans of England and Scotland.

"Without provocation," says Hume, describing the commencement of the outbreak, on the authority of Sir John Temple, " without opposition, the astonished English, living in profound peace and full security, were massacred by their nearest neighbours, with whom they had long upheld a continued intercourse of kindness and good offices." Again : " All the tortures which wanton cruelty could devise—all the lingering pains of body, the anguish of mind, the agonies of despair—could not satiate revenge *excited without injury, and cruelty derived from no cause.*"

What I have to write will expose the grossest exaggeration in this description ; what I have written clearly proves either inexcusable ignorance or falsification on the part of the historian as to the absence of injury and the causelessness of the outbreak. I do not question that very many murders and massacres on a small scale were perpetrated by the Irish during the ten or twelve years of this terrible civil war ; but I maintain that no civil war ever occurred under similar circumstances without similar deplorable consequences; and further, that none ever will occur under similar circumstances without similar outrages, till mankind have learned and reduced to practice the precept, that when smitten on one cheek they shall turn the other to the smiter. I assert also that these Irish outrages were perpetrated by enraged mobs, impelled by what Burke calls "the merciless policy of fear," or by wicked savages, such as exist among all bodies of men. The atrocities in both kinds were liberally retorted by the Government and by the disciplined forces under its control. I will not assert, nor do I think, the atrocities of either side in any degree excusable; but I hold that the atrocities of a rude and ignorant mob are less inexcusable than those of an organised, civilized, and ultra-religious government. I make no terms with cruelty, and impartially abhor it, no matter when, where, by whom or against whom it is perpetrated; even though the perpetrators believe, or pretend to believe, that they murder for the love of God, or to promote the cause of "The immaculate spouse of Christ."*

The rebellion broke out in Ulster on the 23rd of October, 1641, and speedily became general throughout the province. It was a part of the plan of the insurgents to seize upon the Castle of Dublin, and to

---

* The presumptuous and profane name given at this time by the Scottish Covenanters to the Established Church of Scotland.

supply themselves from it with arms and ammunition; but this part of the plot was completely defeated by information conveyed to the Lords Justices (Parsons and Borlase) by Owen O'Connolly, on the night of October the 22nd.

The character of the chief governors powerfully influenced the course of affairs. There is good reason to believe that they adopted measures deliberately with the intention of promoting and extending the rebellion, with a view to consequent confiscations. They were both staunch Puritans; but Borlase was a mere soldier, and was led by Parsons. Parsons was an extremely wicked man.

"This was another most selfish and successful adventurer; and, therefore, very much interested in the extirpation of the native race. He got immense grants of lands in Meath, Cavan, Cork, Tipperary, Limerick, and Fermanagh. He was eventually appointed Surveyor-General, and in this capacity became enormously wealthy."*

The following revolting narrative is abstracted by Cooke Taylor, in his *Civil Wars of Ireland*, from the statement in Carte's *Life of Ormond*:—

"Bryan and Turlough Byrne were the rightful owners of a tract in Leinster, called the Ranelaghs. Its vicinity to the capital made it a desirable plunder; and accordingly Parsons, Lord Esmond, and some others, determined that it should be forfeited. The Byrnes, however, had powerful interest in England, and obtained a patent grant of their lands from the

* The Rev. G. Hill, *The MacDonnells of Antrim*, p. 59, note 38.

King. Parsons and Esmond were not to be disappointed so easily. They flatly refused to pass the royal grant; and, deeming the destruction of the Byrnes necessary to their safety, they had them arrested on a charge of treason. The witnesses provided to support the charge were Duffe, whom Turlough Byrne, as a justice of the peace, had sent to prison for cow-stealing, MacArt and MacGriffin, two notorious thieves, and a farmer named Archer. This last long resisted the attempts to force him to become a perjured witness; and his obstinacy was punished by the most horrible tortures. He was burned in the fleshy parts of the body with hot irons; placed on a gridiron over a charcoal fire; and finally flogged until nature could support him no longer, and he promised to swear anything that the Commissioners pleased. Bills of indictment were presented to two successive grand juries in the County of Carlow, and at once ignored, as the suborned witnesses were unworthy of credit, and contradicted themselves and each other. For this opposition to the will of Government the jurors were summoned to the Star Chamber in Dublin and heavily fined. The witnesses MacArt and MacGriffin, being no longer useful, were given up to the vengeance of the law. They were hanged for robbery at Kilkenny, and with their dying breath declared the innocence of the Byrnes. The ingenuity of Parsons and his accomplices was not yet exhausted. The Byrnes presented themselves before the court of King's Bench in Dublin to answer any charge that might be brought against them. No prosecutor appeared, and yet the Chief Justice refused to grant their discharge. During two years repeated orders were transmitted from England, directing that the Byrnes should be freed from further process, and restored to their estates; but the faction in the Castle evaded and disobeyed every mandate. At length, on learning that the Duke of Richmond, the generous patron of the persecuted Irishmen, was dead, it was determined by Parsons to complete the destruction of the victims. He had before been baffled by the integrity of a grand jury; on this occasion he took proper precautions to prevent a similar disappointment. The bills were sent before the grand jurors of Wicklow, the majority of whom had obtained grants of the Byrne property, and all were intimately connected with the prosecutors. The evidence placed before this impartial body was the depositions of four criminals, who were pardoned on condition of giving evidence; but even these wretches were not brought in person before the jury. Their depositions were taken in Irish by one of the prosecutors, and translated by one of his creatures. These suspicious documents, however, proved sufficient, and the bills were found.

"To procure additional evidence, it was necessary to use expedients still more atrocious. A number of persons were seized and subjected to the mockery of trial by martial law, though the regular courts were sitting. The most horrid tortures were inflicted on those who refused to accuse the Byrnes; and some of the most obstinate were punished with death. But the firmness of the victims presented obstacles which were not overcome before some virtuous Englishmen represented the affair so strongly to the King that he was shamed into interference. He sent over Commissioners from England to investigate the entire affair. The Byrnes were brought before them and honourably acquitted. Their lives were thus saved; but Parsons had previously contrived to obtain a great portion of their estates by patent, and was permitted to keep them undisturbed.

"This narrative, which has been rather softened in its horrible details, may appear to many too shocking to be believed; but all the documents are still preserved in the library of the Dublin University, and it is circumstantially related by Carte, a historian remarkable for his hostility to the Irish."

Owen O'Connolly was immediately despatched with information respecting the insurrection to the Lord Lieutenant, the Earl of Leinster, which was forthwith communicated to the English Houses of Parliament.

Sir John Temple and Lord Clarendon are the historians from whom, in an especial manner, most Protestants have taken the accounts they give of the atrociously inhuman proceedings of the rebels. Hume continually quotes Temple; and I cannot deny that he had apparently good reason to trust his narrative. Certainly nothing short of the strongest facts could discredit his and Clarendon's testimony. Temple, who was Master of the Rolls in Ireland, and a Privy Councillor, published his history within a few years of the outbreak. He had the best opportunities for procuring reliable information respecting the conduct of the insurgents, and saw with his own eyes in Dublin some of the deplorable consequences of it. Clarendon also enjoyed most unusual opportunities for procuring correct information. Temple's testimony is that 150,000 Protestants were slaughtered in the first two months of the rebellion; Clarendon's, that 40,000 or 50,000 were slain before they had any suspicion of their danger.

Mr. Froude gives the following statement in the beginning of his account of the rebellion:—

"On December the 1st—I am particular about these dates, because it is insisted that the story of the massacre was an afterthought, made up in the following year to justify the confiscation of the estates of the insurgents—on December the 1st a petition [probably written a fortnight before] was presented to the English Parliament, signed by the Irish Council, stating that there were then 40,000 rebels in the field. 'Their tyranny,' says this document, 'is so great, that they put both man, woman, and child that are Protestants to the sword, not sparing either age, sex, degree, or reputation. They have stripped naked many Protestants, and so sent them to the city, men and women. They have ravished many virgins and women before their husbands' faces, and taken their children and dashed their brains against the walls in the sight of their parents, and at length destroyed them likewise without pity or humanity.'

"On December the 14th the following letter from Ireland was read in the English Parliament: 'All I can tell you is the miserable state we continue under, for the rebels daily increase in men and munition in all parts, except the province of Munster, exercising all manner of cruelties, and striving who can be most barbarously exquisite in tormenting the poor Protestants, cutting off their ears, fingers, and hands, plucking out their eyes, boiling the hands of the little children before their mothers' faces, stripping women naked, and ripping them up.'

"On the 12th of December, 1641, Sir John Temple writes to Charles, at this time in Edinburgh, as follows, respecting the atrocious proceedings he attributes to the rebels:—' Thus enraged, and armed by these pretences, they march on, furiously destroying all the English, sparing neither sex nor age throughout the kingdom, most barbarously murdering them, and that with greater cruelty than ever was yet used among Turks and infidels. I will not trouble your Majesty with the sad story of our miseries here. Many thousands of our nation are already perished under their cruel hands, and the poor remainder of them go up and down, desolate, naked, and most miserably afflicted with cold and hunger, all inns and other places in the country being prohibited, under penalties, to entertain or give any kind of relief to them, so as here we sit, wearied out with the most lamentable and fearful outcries of our poor distressed countrymen, and have no means to afford them any redress, nor indeed any great hopes long to preserve ourselves and this city from the fury of the rebels, who threaten us with ruin and desolation.'" (Froude, *English in Ireland*, vol. i., p. 105.)

I request especial attention to the circumstances that the two first of these documents were addressed to a body at a safe distance from the scene of the manufactured atrocities, of which the Puritan majority were greedy to hear, and prepared to believe any tale of barbarities perpetrated by Irish savages and idolators.

It is now my turn to call, like Mr. Froude, special attention to the date, but to the authorship also, of the following document, addressed, not to strangers in London, but to gentlemen residing among the barbarians, and consequently well aware of whatever excesses they had been guilty of. The date of the following commission is December the 23rd, 1641, at which time Temple asserts that 150,000 Protestant throats had been cut in Ulster; Lord Clarendon, 40,000 or 50,000; and it was issued by the same Lords Justices who presented to the Long Parliament the first of the three documents just quoted.

| "A Commission to diverse eminent Protestant clergymen in Ireland to take examinations on oath concerning the Irish rebellion. Dated: December 23rd, A.D. 1641. | "CHARLES, by the Grace of God, King of England, France, and Ireland, Defender of the Faith, etc. "To our well-beloved Henry Jones, Dean of Kilmore, Roger Puttock, William Hitchcock, Randal Adams, John Sterne, William Aldrich, Henry Brereton, and John Watsons, greeting. |

"Whereas divers wicked and disloyal people have lately risen in arms in this kingdom, and robbed and spoiled many of our good subjects, British and Protestants, who have been separated from their several habitations, and scattered in most lamentable manner; and forasmuch as it is needful to take due examination concerning the same, know ye that we, reposing special trust and confidence in your care, diligence, and provident circumspection, have nominated you to be our Commissioners, and do hereby give unto you, or any two or more of you, full power and authority, from time to time to call before you, and examine upon oath on the holy Evangelists (which hereby we authorise you, or any two or more of you to administer, as well to all such persons as have been robbed and despoiled, as to all witnesses that can give testimony therein) what robberies and spoils have been committed on them since the 22nd of October last, or shall hereafter be committed on them, or any of them; what the particulars were or are, whereof they were or shall be so robbed and spoiled; to what value, by whom, and what their names are, and where they now or last dwelt who committed those robberies; and on what day or night the said robberies or spoils were committed or done; what traitorous or disloyal words, speeches or actions were then, or at any other time, uttered or committed by those robbers, or any of them, and how often; and all other circumstances concerning the said particulars, and every of them: And you, our said Commissioners, are to reduce to writing all the examinations which you, or any two or more of you, shall take as aforesaid; and the same to return to our justices and council of our realm of Ireland, under the hands and seals of any two or more of you, as aforesaid.

"Witness our right trusty and well-beloved Counsellors, Sir William Parsons, Knight and Baronet, and Sir John Borlace, Knight, our Justices of our said realm of Ireland.

"Dublin, the 23rd of December, in the seventeenth year of our reign."

The scandalous calumny and falsehood which this commission renders patent, in the letter bearing date about a month earlier than this, of the Lords Justices to the English Parliament, makes it a difficult matter for me to express my indignation in decorous terms. It may, perhaps, be said that they were themselves misled by evidence given them by terrified, stripped, and starving fugitives. If so, where is their letter to the Commons, retracting their calumny? There is no such letter.

"Never sure," says Counsellor Candour, who is made to plead in favour of the Irish Roman Catholics in Mr. Brooke's excellent *Tryal of the Cause of the Roman Catholics; on a Special Commission, directed to Lord Chief Justice Reason, Lord Chief Baron Interest, and Mr. Justice Clemency, Wednesday, August 5th,* 1761: " Never, sure, was a more minute inquiry enjoined to be made by Protestants of damages done to Protestants: it reaches even to the treason of words and circumstances. But is there any inquiry enjoined here concerning murder, or are any such murders intimated, or supposed to have been committed before the issuing of this commission? The Protestants, it is true, are here said to have been robbed and spoiled, and driven from their habitations, and scattered abroad; but they are called together again, with their adherents and witnesses, to be examined, *vivâ voce* as one would imagine, touching the damages they had suffered; a pretty strong implication that they had not been murdered. For otherwise it should seem that a commission to inquire into the murder as well as the spoil of 150,000 ought to have been directed to such magistrates as Æacus and Rhadamanthus, who might have authority to take the depositions of the deceased."

Soon, however, numerous murders—especially of the clergy of the Established and Presbyterian churches, who, with the exception of the truly Christian Bedell, had exasperated the people by the stinging abuse and contempt they thought it their duty to pour forth continually on the cherished religion of the Celtic Irish—and many partial massacres were perpetrated by mobs of peasants, called soldiers, under the leading of Sir Phelim O'Neill, an inhuman leader, without doubt; yet even he shot his foster-brother (equivalent, in the eyes of the Irish of that time, to the putting to death of his brother by blood) on account of his having killed Lord Caulfield, then a prisoner in Sir Phelim's custody.

The treatment of the expelled English and Scotch by the insurgents was extremely inhuman. In the November of an unusually severe winter the Protestants were often stripped naked, and driven out without food, to make the best of their way to the nearest place of refuge. No doubt many children, women, and old men must have perished of cold and hunger; and, assuredly, all of these deaths are fairly to be added to the number of those persons who were directly murdered or massacred. Great numbers of the fugitives died also, after reaching places of refuge, by famine and its consequent pestilence; but for these deaths I hold England and Scotland responsible, whose barbarous apathy in not sending immediate military aid, arms, food, and means of transport across the channel to their wretched countrymen, was unintelligibly and revoltingly heartless. Even with regard to the numbers who must have died on their way to places of safety, and in those places, there is as usual great exaggeration. The Protestants had possession of Drogheda in Louth. In Cavan the palace and cathedral of Bishop Bedell, even the graveyard, afforded protection to many. In Fermanagh, Enniskillen; in Tyrone, Omagh, Newtownstewart, and Augher Castle; in Donegall, Ballyshannon, Lifford, and Letterkenny; in Derry, the City of Londonderry and Coleraine; in the County Antrim, Larne, Antrim, Carrickfergus, Belfast, and Lisburn; and in Downshire, Newtownards, and Downpatrick, were all held throughout the war by the Protestants. I do not believe that any of the fugitives were more than thirty miles distant from a place of refuge.

But it must not be supposed that the Irish had a monopoly of massacre and murder. Scotch troops from Carrickfergus perpetrated a very shocking massacre, on Sunday, January the 9th, 1642, in the neighbouring Island-Magee, a peninsula running out some five or six miles between Larne Lough and the North Channel. There is no dispute as to the massacre; but the Roman Catholic writers contend that this was the first massacre perpetrated in Ulster, and that those perpetrated by the Irish were retaliatory. The Protestant authorities insist, on the contrary, that the Island-Magee massacre was provoked by previous Irish massacres, and a hot controversy on this subject was long carried on between the parties. Dr. Reid, a very painstaking and usually accurate historian *(History of the Presbyterian Church in Ireland)* asserts that this massacre was retaliatory, and that there were no Scotch soldiers in Carrickfergus for three months after the date of it. The massacre by the Irish alluded to was perpetrated by a mob about forty miles from Carrickfergus, on the 4th of January, 1642, when, more than two months after the 23rd of October, 1641, there was not, according to Temple, a surviving Protestant to carry the report of it, but when in truth there were few or none of the survivors who had not fled to Coleraine, Carrickfergus, or Belfast. Dr. Reid was either ignorant of the fact or forgot it, that Charles sent from Scotland to the north of Ulster, in the very beginning of the insurrection, 1,500 men of the lately disbanded Scottish army.* I have no direct authority to say that these men were landed at Carrickfergus; but I do not doubt it. They might have been landed at Dundalk, Carlingford, Newry, Coleraine, or Derry; but the three first-named towns were then in possession of the insurgents, and till June, 1642. In Derry the inhabitants were organizing a force from among themselves for their defence; and Coleraine, a few days later, was besieged by a tumultuary force of ten or twelve hundred men, under Alaster McDonnell, who would have been

* Wright's *History of Ireland*, vol. i., p. 679.

driven like chaff before the wind by 1,500 Scottish soldiers, if they had been in the town.

I therefore conclude, as the French say, "*par voie d'exclusion*," that Charles's force was sent to Carrickfergus, and were the perpetrators of the Island-Magee massacre. The controversy on this subject has, however, been put to rest by direct testimony, with which Dr. Reid could not have been acquainted. *A History of the Warr of Ireland from* 1641 *to* 1653, by a British officer of the regiment of Sir John Clotworthy, afterwards Lord Massarene, has been lately published, which occasionally throws light on the transactions of these times.

"I remember," says he, "about Christmas that winter of the warrs [1641] there came to us at Antrim, with their captain, one Lindsay, a civil man, who loved no murder, out of . . . . the number of about forty horsemen as a troop, and had a horn for a trumpet, all living about Tullahogue [near Dungannon, in the County Tyrone], who left their wives and children, with their goods, with the enemy, who all concluded they were all destroyed, and in revenge they could not endure to see any Irishman; but they must beat him to destroy him. So one night they left Antrim, their garrison, unknown to all their officers but their own lieutenant, Barnet Lindsay, and fell on Mr. Upton's tenants, a gentleman who hated to see or hear of innocent blood drawn, and would save them if he could, but was then in Carrickfergus; and they murdered about eighty persons, men, women, and children, near Templepatrick, at which other Scotts took example, and did the like in Island-Magee. Then the Irish, on the other side, in the County of Antrim, to be revenged, spared not to destroy the Scottish where they could get advantage, as at . . . Such was the fury of both Scotts and Irish for blood and revenge that they thought it good service to God to destroy one another; as indeed it continued so till in May the Scottish army came out of Scotland, consisting of 10,000 soldiers, at least by that name, under the command of General Leslie and his Major-General Munroe, and until Owen MacArt [Owen Roe O'Neill] came over from beyond seas, and was Captain-General of the Irish of Ulster, who both gave fair quarters like soldiers, and halted these inhumane acts before done."

" As for the number of the British murdered the first winter of the wars, I will acquaint the reader with the same as far as I could learn, after scrutiny made into the same as I said before. The most was committed in Ulster, and it did not exceed through all Ulster above the sixtieth part held forth by those authors I named before."

In July Sir John Clotworthy sailed across Lough Neagh with 500 men, and took Fort Mountjoy, near Dungannon, in Tyrone, without opposition.

" Here," says the author just quoted, " there came to us daily women and children of the British, so much that they were sent away the first fair wind to Antrim, for they could not be maintained [viz., at Mountjoy]; and some of which were the wives and children of that troop was mentioned before, who gave them up for lost and drew much innocent blood in revenge of them."

This, so far as I know, was the first massacre perpetrated in the County Antrim. It had, at least, the bad excuse that the perpetrators believed their own wives and children had been slaughtered. I think it of very small consequence which party began the massacres. Both had now " screwed their courage" to the massacring point, and as to which should shed the first blood, this was a matter of mere chance; but my narrative proves that Dr. Reid was mistaken, both as to who committed the first massacre in the County of Antrim, and as to the fact that there were Scotch soldiers in Carrickfergus at the time of it. Dr. Reid's account of the military surprise and slaughter of sixty or eighty soldiers, and subsequent massacre by a mob is thus described by him *(History of Presbyterianism in Ireland,* vol. i., p. 324) :—

"On the morning of Monday, the 3d of January [1642] a party of Irish rebels, from both sides of the river Bann, headed by Alaster MacDonnell,* (Colkittagh), surprised a detachment of British stationed at Portna [on the Bann, about five miles from Ballymoney and the same distance from Ballymena], near Kilrea, under the command of Captains Fergus McDougall, Peebles, and Glover, and massacred between sixty and eighty of them in their beds."

Mr. Froude misquotes Dr. Reid, and thus scandalously calumniates Alaster McDonnell, as follows :—

---

\* I am bound both by clanship and kinship to vindicate, so far as I can with truth, the calumniated character of this remarkable man. He is the "Colkitto" of Milton's sonnet. The poet had been ridiculed on account of a rather absurd name (*Tetrachordon*) which he had given to a book lately published by him.

> "Why, is it," he says, "harder, sirs, than Gordon,
> Colkitto, or Macdonnel, or Galasp?
> These rugged names to our like mouths grow sleek,
> That would have made Quinctilian stare and gasp."

Newton, in his edition of Milton, conjectures that the two last names, MacDonnell or Galasp, were those of Presbyterian clergymen. I have no doubt the three last belong to Alaster. Col or Colla Kittagh (Col the left-handed) was his father's name; his grandfather's was Gillaspie (Archibald), Milton's Galasp. It was usual in the Highlands of Scot-

"Alaster MacDonnell had destroyed some English families in their beds at Kilrea. Seventy or eighty old men, women, and children had been killed by the same party near Ballintoy and Oldstown. On the Sunday following, a party of the expelled farmers, maddened by their losses, accompanied by a few soldiers from Carrickfergus, in revenge slew thirty Catholics in Island-Magee."

Dr. Reid's account is true. Mr. Froude converts the slaughter of soldiers in a night attack into a massacre of men, women, and children. There is not a shadow of evidence that Alaster McDonnell had any concern in the immediately subsequent massacres of women and children, and the burning of Ballymoney; and the testimony of the officer of Sir John Clotworthy's regiment refutes the statement regarding the Island-Magee atrocity.

The following narrative is requisite to account for Alaster's night attack on the soldiers at Portna. Lord Antrim was a Roman Catholic, and a staunch Royalist all his life. He was a personal friend of Charles, and

---

land, to ensure the identity of a person named, to add one or more of the person's immediate forefathers, and accordingly Alaster was often designated as Alaster MacColl, MacGillaspie, MacColl Dhu, Mac, etc. (Alexander, the son of Coll, son of Archibald, son of Black Coll, etc.) Sir Walter Scott says, in the *Legend of Montrose*, that he was a Scottish islander. His father was certainly born in Ireland, but owned the islands of Colonsa, Oronsa, Staffa, and Iona, and was at this time, by the death of Sir James McDonnell, without issue, chief of the old family of Isla Cantyre and the Glens. Argyle, Gillaspie Grumach (Ill-favoured Archibald) was now using his best endeavours to drive this family out of Scotland, in which he succeeded, and would have entirely extinguished it but for the retreat they had in the County Antrim.

a favourite of Henrietta Maria. He was one of the richest landholders in Ireland in 1641. He married in 1636, in his father's lifetime, while Lord Dunluce, Catherine Manners, one of the richest ladies in England. She was daughter and heiress of Lord De Ros, afterwards Earl of Rutland, and widow of George Villiers, the murdered Duke of Buckingham, who left her richly dowered; yet their faithful devotion to the royal cause had reduced them to beggary in 1648. In a letter in cypher, dated 18th February, 1648, to Cardinal Panzirolo, Rinuccini, the Pope's Nuncio in Ireland, writes :—

"The Duchess of Buckingham, now the wife of the Marquis of Antrim, who formerly testified the liveliest zeal for the Catholic religion, has absolutely no means of support, save six hundred livres granted her by the Supreme Council. As it is very difficult to get in this sum, the poor lady, on the departure of her husband for France, was reduced to ask the loan of two hundred crowns, which I immediately advanced to her. But as I much doubt its being repaid, and perhaps shall be obliged to assist her again, I think it advisable to acquaint your Eminence, and I trust that the disposal in this charitable act of a part of the Papal subsidy will be approved by his Holiness, of whose benevolence this lady is truly worthy, and I shall endeavour to act in the case so that no trouble or difficulty shall accrue to his Holiness."

Archibald Stewart, head of a family that had migrated from Bute to Ballintoy, in the County Antrim, in the reign of Elizabeth, was appointed Lord Antrim's agent—or, as Strafford calls him, "his man"—in 1630.

Shortly before the outbreak of 1641, Stewart was employed by Lord Antrim to raise a regiment, which, it need not be said, he intended for the support of Charles. The regiment, however, which Stewart raised, consisted of 600 Scottish Presbyterians, of course staunch Parliamentarians, 100 Highland Roman Catholics, under Alaster McColl, and 100 Irish Roman Catholics, under one of the O'Cahans, of Dunseverick Castle, beside the Giant's Causeway, the ruins of which still exist. These 200 Catholics were of course staunch Royalists. As soon as the time for action arrived, this regiment naturally and inevitably fell into two factions, each earnestly desirous of cutting the throats of the other at the first opportunity; as naturally and inevitably as a regiment formed at the present time of 600 Antrim Orangemen and 200 Kerry Fenians would, in the event of a struggle to separate Ireland from England, fall into two factions athirst each for the other's blood.

I have no authority for asserting that Stewart was guilty of treachery to his employer on this occasion; but the circumstances led his enemies strongly to suspect it.

The Presbyterians and the Irish and Highlanders had now been scowling at one another for some months; their mutual hatred had had time to ferment and acquire spiritual strength; and, no doubt, the former had exasperated the latter by frequent assurances that they were on a quick march, by a *facilis descensus* along "the primrose path to the everlasting bonfire;" while the latter, with less taste for polemics, were no less confident that the Presbyterians were speeding down that very path, minus the primroses, but "with thorns also and thistles" instead. In the beginning of 1642 the time for active measures had arrived. McDonnell and O'Cahan had, no doubt, anxiously debated the matter between themselves. "We are one to three against those villain Roundheads, and have no chance in an open-field fight. We must proceed by stratagem. We must trap them in a wooded defile, attack them by a night surprise, or, etc."

They chose the surprise, and with the result related above. Dr. Reid represents Alaster McColl as "one of the chiefs of that party" [the Roman Catholic], and asserts that "a party of horse were despatched from Carrickfergus to apprehend this influential Romanist."[*] He quotes no authority, and I know of none for either statement. What is certain is that Alaster was at this time a young man quite unknown to fame, and Stewart plainly shows that he did not share Reid's mistake, by the appointment which he considered suitable to Alaster's merits and claims—the command of a company in the Antrim regiment. He is often spoken of as a near relation, sometimes as a brother of Lord Antrim.

[*] Reid, vol. i., p. 314.

Lord Antrim's grandfather and Alaster's great grandfather were brothers. They were consequently second cousins once removed.

Alaster, however, rapidly acquired name and fame. Stewart had

"Placed garrisons, principally composed of Scots, in the house and church of Ballintoy [near the Giant's Causeway] under Mr. Fullarton and Mr. Archibald Boyd; in the Castle of Oldstone, near Clough [four or five miles from Ballymena], under Mr. Walter Kennedy; and in such other parts through the open country as might most effectually check the incursions of the rebels."* "Immediately after the slaughter at Portnaw, Alaster proceeded to attack the Castle of Oldstone, which was the property of Donald Gorm [Blue-eyed] McDonnell. McDonnell's force was joined, when near the castle, by that under Art Oge O'Neill, of the family of the last three lords of that name, who was the first to summon Kennedy to surrender. Kennedy concluded that under the circumstances 'discretion was the better part of valour;' but with even more than an ordinary amount of discretion he replied to Art Oge's summons—that he 'would never surrender to an O'Neill a castle that belonged to a MacDonnell.' Kennedy, a cannie Scot, took care, of course, the words were spoken so as to be heard by Alaster MacColl, and the latter was so flattered by the reply that he swore to Kennedy by the cross on his sword that provided the castle was peacefully surrendered, the garrison would be permitted to pass out in safety, and that the multitude of non-combatants, who had sought refuge therein, might carry away all their effects and retire to their own houses. This was more than Kennedy could have hoped for. He surrendered, therefore, without delay, and, so far as MacDonnell was concerned, or had the means of controlling others, the terms of surrender were faithfully carried out."†

\* Reid, vol. i., p. 314.
† Rev. G. Hill's *MacDonnells of Antrim*, p. 4.

Mr. Hill adds, in a note :—

"After the surrender, however, several persons were said to have been massacred by a mob. The victims, including women and children, were making their way towards Larne or Carrickfergus, when they were attacked on the side of the Ravel water, by a murderous gang, led by one Toole MacHugh O'Hara. MacSkimin gives this statement on the authority of one of the 'depositions' preserved in the library of Trinity College, Dublin." As for the other massacre under the walls of Oldstone Castle, mentioned by Dr. Reid, I know of no other authority for it but his, and there is not a vestige of evidence that Alaster MacColl had any knowledge of or concern in either of them.*

* "The O'Haras in all their branches were among the most active and cruel of the Irish insurgents in the Route [an extensive district in the North of the County Antrim] during 1641. After the surrender of Clough Castle, many women and children who had been permitted by the MacDonnells to go safely away to Larne, were followed and massacred on the banks of the Glenravel water by a fellow named O'Hara, son of a Hugh O'Hara, and, no doubt, connected with some of the families of that name then so numerous in the parishes of Lough Guile and Ballymoney."—See McSkimin's *History of Carrickfergus*, 3rd Edition, p. 46. [Hill's *Stewarts of Ballintoy*, p. 16, note *ad finem.*]

"The insurgents in the County Derry forthwith crossed the Bann, under a leader named John Mortimer, and united their forces with those of Alaster MacDonnell and Tirlough Oge O'Cahan. From Portnaw they marched to the residence of Sir James Macdonnell [Sir James McDonnell was great grandson of Sorley Buy, and therefore he and Lord Antrim were second cousins once removed], who dwelt at the Vow, in the parish of Finvoy. They were joined by such of his tenants as were able to carry arms, and also by the tenants of Donnell Gorm MacDonnell, of Killoquin, in the parish of Rasharkin.

"In the meantime, the Irish inhabitants on both sides of the Bann, fearing Archibald Stewart and such soldiers as he could collect, in the absence of McDonnell, O'Cahan, and Mortimer, assembled in multitudes, with their wives and children, burned a little town which then stood at the Cross, near Ballymoney, and afterwards burned Ballymoney, slaying all the British inhabitants they could lay hands on, without distinction of age or sex. Thus the mere mob, frightened and

Archibald Stewart had betaken himself, with a remnant of his regiment, after the slaughter at Portnaw, to Coleraine, and had recruited his force, probably by fugitives in that town able to bear arms, to about eight hundred men, and McDonnell occupied Ballymoney, where he had raised his force to about the same number. Stewart marched from Coleraine on the 10th of February to attack the insurgents. McDonnell encountered him on the following day at a place called the Laney, within a mile of Ballymoney. He received

---

frenzied by the prevailing excitement, did actually more damage to life and property than the regularly organised forces of the insurgents." [Hill's *Stewarts of Ballintoy*, p. 12.]

" Whilst the mob were burning the village of Cross and the town of Ballymoney, the regularly disciplined force, which had deserted from Mr. Stewart, was led by the two MacDonnells, James and Alaster MacColl, against the Castle of Clough, defended by Walter Kennedy. After the capture of this place, James MacDonnell wrote the following letter to Mr. Stewart, whom he addresses as cousin, and who must have been in Coleraine when he received it. This letter is preserved in the MS. volume already mentioned, at F. 3, 9. 3402 :—

" Cosen Archebald, I receaved your letter, and, to tell the truth, I was ever of that opinion, and so were the most of all these gentlemen ; that your owne selfe had no ―――― in you ; but certainly had I not begun when I did, I and all these gentlemen, with wiffe and children had been utterly destroyed ; of which I gott intelligence from one that heard the plot a laying ; and those captains of yours (whom I may call rather cowboyes) were, every daye, vexing ourselves and our tenants, of purpose to pick quarrells, which no flesh was able to endure ; and judge you whether I had reason to prevent such mischefe ; and I vow to the Almighty, had they not thus forst me, as they did many others besides me that would rather hang than goe on as they did, I would stick as firm to your side as any of yourselves ; though I confesse it would be the worse thinge for me and mine that ever I sawe. To speak to you really the truth, and the true information of the whole kingdome, upon my creditt I now doe it ; all the whole kingdome in

a disastrous defeat, his force being nearly annihilated; and McDonnell became at once a distinguished leader. The day of the battle was known long after among the Presbyterians in the Route as Black Friday. The Rev. Mr. Clogy, stepson-in-law of Bishop Bedell, speaking of this battle, bestows on Alaster a pedigree much more ancient than that claimed by "the gentlemen of his haughty sirname," as Sir Walter Scott calls them. He deduces Alaster from Anak, of whom and his gigantic sons, the spies that Moses had sent before him to Canaan, had reported that the Hebrews were, in comparison, "as grasshoppers."

generall are of our side, except Dublin, whoe hath 20,000 men about, in leager of it, if it be not now taken; Drogheda whoe hath 16,000 men about it, and are these ten dayes past eatinge of horse-flesh; Carrickefergus, Coulraine, and my lord of Claneboys, and my lo of the Ardes; this is the truth on my credit; ballemeanagh, Antrim, and all the garrisons between this and Carrickefergus are all fled to Carrickefergus; soe that it is but a folly to resist what God pleeseth to happen; but certainly they will have all Ireland presently, whatever time they keep it. You may truly inform my friends in Coulraine that I would wish they ———, and if they yeild me the towne it shall be good for them and me, for the booty shall be myne, and they shall be sure of good quarters; for I will send for all the Raghlin boates to Portrush and from thanes [thence] send all the people away into Scotland, wch, if it be not done before Sir Phelim is [his] army comes to the towne, who comes the next week ——— thousand men and piece of artillery, all my desire of doing them good will be to no purpose; therefore send me word what you doe therein; as for both your houses they shall be safe, and so should all the houses in the country if they would be persuaded by me; the Oldstowe [Oldstone, now Clough] was rendered me, and all they within had good quarters, only the Clandebayes souldours and the two regiments from beyon the Ban were a little greedy for pillaginge, which could not be helpt. As for killing of women none of my souldiers dare do it for his life, but the common people that are not under rule doth it in spite of

"The Scotts then," says Mr. Clogy, "throughout all the province of Ulster, where they were most numerous, betook themselves to holds, leaving all the open country to the enemy; for the first attempt of Col Kiltach had so frighted them, that they thought no man was able to stand before that son of Anak. In his first encounter with a few Irish Highlanders and some of Antrim's Irish rebels (that were brethren in evil) against eight hundred English and Scots, having commanded these murderers to lay down all their fire-arms, he fell in amongst them with swords and dirks, or sceanes, in such a furious irresistible manner that it was reported that not a man of them escaped of all the eight hundred, the first and greatest loss in battle that we sustained in all that war, save one in Munster (under the unhappy conduct of Sir Charles Vavasour); whereupon the rebels rode in triumph, with their swords drawn, through the streets of Kilkenny, as if they had conquered all England."

The mode of attack, which the man of peace shud-

our teeth; but for your people the killed of women and children and old people about 3 score.——My Lo. and Lady are gone to Slain,* to whom I have sent; tell my bror Hill and Mrs. Barwicke that their people are all in good health, but ——— in my own company.—I desire you not to stirr out of that till I be neere you myselfe, for fear you should fall in the hands of the seaven hundred I have in the lower part of the country, who would give you noe quarter at all; but when I have settled things here, you may come to me yourselfe and your dearest friends to a few, and the rest to transport them with the rest into Scotland; as for goinge againe the King we will dye sooner or my Lo: of Antrim either, but their only aime is to have their religion settled and every one in his own ancient inheritance; thus wishing you to take my counsell which, I protest to God I will give you as really as to myself, and haveing the hope of your beleavinge me herein, I rest your very loveinge coussen still, JAMES MCDONNELL.

"From the Catholick Campe at Oldstone, the 11th of Jan., 1641" [old style].

*"Sir James McDonnell refers to the departure of Lord Antrim and his wife, the Duchess of Buckingham, from the castle of Dunluce."— The Rev. Mr. Hill's *Stewarts of Ballintoy*, pp. 13-15. Coleraine, 1865.

ders at, was simply the usual tactic of the Highlanders in battle at this time. Before the charge each clan was formed into a wedge-shaped regiment, the front edge of which was formed of the chief and gentry of the clan, who were always the best armed, and usually the largest and strongest men. Just before the charge they fired into the enemy, threw down their guns, and drawing the broadsword with the right hand and the dirk with the left, rushed upon the foe. Each Highlander carried a small round target on the left forearm. It was his object on reaching his antagonist to throw his bayonet up with this, and dashing in between two men to give the broadsword to one and the dirk to the other. This certainly very formidable mode of attack had the effect, at the Laney, at Killikrankie, at Preston-Pans, and on many another occasion, of scattering the enemy like chaff before the wind. Sir Walter Scott gives a graphic account of it in his description of the battle of Preston-Pans in *Waverley.*

Coleraine and Ballintoy were immediately besieged, and in a few weeks reduced to the last extremity of distress. Great numbers of fugitives had flocked into Coleraine, and over-crowding and starvation produced pestilential fever, by which great numbers of the inhabitants perished. Temple has the hardihood to print the following evidence of James Redferne :—

"The mortality there (in Coleraine) was such and so great, that many thousands died there in two days; and that the

living, though scarce able to do it, laid the carcasses of those
in great ranks into vast and wide holes, laying them so close
and thick as if they had packed herrings together."

The truth was bad and sad enough without such
preposterous exaggeration as this. Sir James McDonnell mentions that Lord Antrim had retired with his
wife from Dunluce to Slane, near Drogheda, in the
beginning of the insurrection. He now returned, says
Carte, in his *Life of Ormond*, vol. i., p. 188,

" To his seat at Dunluce, a strong castle by the seaside; and
after his arrival there, found means to supply Coleraine,
which had been blocked up by the Irish, and was reduced to
extremity, with one hundred beeves, sixty loads of corn, and
other provisions at his own expense."

The Rev. Mr. Hill states :—

" On this occasion Alaster MacColl, who was chief in command, consented so to relax the severity of the siege, that the
inhabitants not only got ample space for themselves and their
cattle, but were supplied with the best descriptions of food,
beef and oatmeal. Alaster MacColl, who had here the fate of
so many Presbyterians literally in his hands, thus dealt with
them very much moré humanely than even the rules of
modern warfare would permit, and certainly very much more
so than the Presbyterians would have dealt with him, had the
circumstances been reversed."*

The same author relates, in his *Stewarts of Ballintoy*, p. 22, another touching instance of humanity on
the part of a truly Christian priest at the siege of Bal-

* *The MacDonnells of Antrim*, p. 72, note 88.

5*

lintoy, which was being prosecuted at the same time as that of Coleraine.

"During these operations," says Mr. Hill, "the adjoining church was crowded with a trembling multitude of women and children, who were every hour threatened with destruction, either by fire or famine. In their dire extremity a good Roman Catholic priest, at great personal risk, interfered for their preservation. With difficulty he obtained permission to bring them water, and, in doing so, filled the water vessels with oatmeal, covering it with a few inches depth of water at the top. In this way he daily carried to the captives as much food as kept them alive till relief came. Tradition states that this truly good Samaritan was called MacGlaime, but nothing is known of him save this one noble Christian act."

From such Christian acts as these arise—

"That incense
Whose fragrance smells to Heaven."

Gladly would I quote any similar deeds of mercy on the part of Parsons or other of the Puritan leaders in Ireland of this time; but as far as I know there are none such to record.

A few weeks later, Monroe, who had arrived in Carrickfergus in April with 2,500 Scotch troops, and had expelled the insurgents from Newry, marched to Coleraine, burning Glenarm on his way, and making Lord Antrim a prisoner at Dunluce. Carte says this was effected in a treacherous manner after an entertainment given him by Lord Antrim; but other authorities deny the treachery. Till lately I had lost sight of Alaster MacColl completely for near two years after this—neither any historical account nor family tradition giving me any information about him between the time when he retreated into the County of Derry, before Monroe's overwhelming force, and the time of his appointment as Major-General of about 2,000 men, despatched by Lord Antrim in the middle of 1644, in aid of Montrose in the Highlands of Scotland. From Sir John Clotworthy's officer, already quoted, I have learned that Alaster quickly united his force with Sir Phelim O'Neill's, who, thus reinforced, marched to the Lagan, a district in the north of the County of Donegall, between the rivers Foyle and Swilly, to attack a body of Protestants under Sir Robert and Sir William Stewart. O'Neill received a severe defeat.

"The next Boute the Irish and British," says this author, "had in Ulster was at a place called Glommaquin,* in the County of Dungall, whither Sir Phelim O'Neil and O'Cahan, their chief commanders, marched with about 4,000 men. Which the British hearing, under the command of Sir Robert Stewart, an old soldier, entrenched themselves in the night, but had not time to make it full breast high before morning, when the Irish appeared close to them, and sent a brigade under the command of Alexander MacColla MacDonnell, a stout brave fellow (under the command of Mount Rose afterwards in Scotland), who charged up alone to the work but was shot, and after a very sharp skirmish the Irish fell back,

---

* Glenmaquin, in the parish of Raphoe, near Lifford, capital of the County of Donegall. The battle was fought 16th June, 1642. Hill—*MacDonnells of Antrim*, p. 75.

and took the retreat, where many were slain, and with much ado O'Cahan brought off MacDonnell in a horse-litter."

His wound was very severe and he had a tedious recovery, during which he was nursed by a priest named O'Crilly.

### III.

In every history of this war which I have met with, scant justice is done to Lord Antrim, in respect to the services he rendered in support of the Royalist cause. He is held up to contempt as a braggart who made magnificent promises in 1644 to raise 10,000 men in aid of Montrose in Scotland, and ended by sending twelve or fifteen hundred men to join his standard in the Highlands. I assert with confidence that Antrim's services to Charles were far more important than those of any other Irish nobleman, with, perhaps, the exception of Ormond. I say perhaps, for I think Ormond's surrender of Dublin to the Long Parliament has left an indelible stain upon his character as a staunch and faithful cavalier. Already, in 1641, Lord Antrim had raised a regiment of 800 men, certainly intended by him for the support of Charles; but, by some unexplained cause, 600 of these men were Presbyterians, and therefore Parliamentarians, at the head of whom, reinforced by 200 volunteers of Coleraine, Archibald Stewart, Lord Antrim's agent, whom he had employed to raise the regiment, marched out to attack Alaster McDonnell, with the result mentioned above.

I do not doubt that Lord Antrim, in offering to raise 10,000 men, much over-rated his power in 1644. His influence in his County of Antrim estate, running from Larne to the north coast and from the Bann to the North Channel, was seriously crippled by the presence of 10,000 Scottish soldiers, under Monroe, at Carrickfergus; and by the Plantation Protestants, under Sir Robert and Sir William Stewart, in the Counties of Derry and Tyrone. A few years before this, the chief of his family, known in the Highlands as the Clandonald South, or the Clan Ian Vohr, which had been for more than a century by much the most powerful family in the Clan MacDonald, had been driven out of Scotland by James and the Campbells; and here, therefore, the influence of Antrim to raise men was impaired by time and absence. Nevertheless, we shall see that he performed much more in recruiting Montrose's force than his depreciators gave him credit for. In Antrim he raised 2,500 men. In June, 1644, he writes to Ormond—

"That he had sent off about 1,600 men, being as many as the ships could conveniently hold, completely armed by his own shifts, besides 1,500 pikes, and that he had discharged 700 or 800 men for want of shipping."* And Ormond himself writes on the 17th of the next month : " The number

* Carte's *Ormond.*

of men embarked by him (Lord Antrim) from Waterford and other places amounted to 2,500, well armed and victualled for two months.* It cannot be denied," says Lord Clarendon, who was no friend of Lord Antrim, "that the levies the Marquis of Antrim made and sent over to Scotland, under the command of Colkitto, were the foundation of all those wonderful acts which were performed afterwards by the Marquis of Montrose. And the Marquis of Montrose did always acknowledge that the rise and beginning of his good success was due and to be imputed to that body of the Irish which had in the beginning been sent him by the Marquis of Antrim; to whom the King had acknowledged the service in several letters of his own handwriting."

In fact, these half-disciplined but heroic County of Antrim peasants formed the backbone of Montrose's force up to the time of the battle of Kilsyth; and in bravery and endurance of hardship and fatigue in a winter's campaign through the snowy Grampians and mountains of Badenoch, Lochaber, and Cantyre, they exhibited a heroism worthy of the hero that led them, speaking of whom, Cardinal de Retz says:—

"Montrose, a Scottish nobleman, head of the house of Graham, the only man in the world that has ever realised to me the idea of certain heroes whom we now discover nowhere but in the lives of Plutarch."

Montrose led these men from victory to victory, from August, 1644, to August, 1645, when the victory of Kilsyth made him master of the open country of Scotland, "from Maidenkirk to John O'Groat's," till

* Carte, vol. iii., p. 328.

the disaster of Philiphaugh. That the exploits of these noble fellows (who perished to a man in battles, or by two massacres, the "thwart disnatured" offspring of Scottish clerical bigotry, which is the purest, the most inhuman, and the most detestable the world has ever seen), are so completely ignored by the Irish historians of this period, is, in my opinion, highly discreditable to them. I propose to redress this wrong, by recording the prowess of these men, the narrative of which strictly belongs to the history of the Irish War of 1641-'52.

On two several occasions Montrose despatched Alaster McDonnell to the western Highlands and Isles to raise recruits among the MacDonalds and their ancient and faithful allied Clans, and he returned bringing along with him seven or eight thousand as fine born-soldiers as ever drew broadsword. It is but fair to attribute a good share of this success to the influence of the names of Antrim and his kinsman Alaster amongst their clansmen.

The Irish auxiliaries landed at Ardnamurchan, in Argyleshire, on the 5th of July, 1644. In crossing the Irish Sea and North Channel they encountered and captured two ships of the Covenant under Colonel Munro, carrying supplies to the Scottish troops in Ulster. Alaster's treatment of his prisoners gives another practical refutation of the character for inhumanity bestowed upon him by Reid and Froude. He released them all except three preachers, whom he retained in the hope of exchanging them for his father, Colkitto, and his two brothers, at this time imprisoned by Argyle. Soon after landing, Alaster took the castles of Mingarry and Kinlochaline, marched coastwise as far as Kintail, and then, having failed completely to kindle the smouldering loyalty of the clans he visited (he was still young and little known among them, and certainly the Rev. Mr. Clogy's terrific account of the battle of the Laney had not yet reached them) he returned in a south-westerly direction, crossing Lochaber and Badenoch, in the hope of hearing of or meeting Montrose. In the meantime Montrose had reached the Highlands on the verge of the Grampians, having at great risk crossed the Lowlands in the disguise of a groom riding a sorry nag and leading a spare horse behind Sir William Rollock and Colonel Sibbald accoutred as covenanting troopers. Amongst other dangers they encountered,—

"They were suddenly accosted by a Scotchman who had served under the Earl of Newcastle, and who was well acquainted with the person of Montrose. Against the scrutiny of the old campaigner no masquerade was availing. The Marquis's 'quick and piercing eye' and 'singular grace in riding' were not to be disguised; and the soldier, passing the pretended officers, at once addressed himself to their servant, and respectfully saluted him by his title. In vain did the latter endeavour to evade the compliment and sustain his part. 'What,' exclaimed the other, still preserving the utmost respect in his countenance and manner, 'Do I not know my

Lord Marquis of Montrose? Go your way, and God be with you wheresoever you go.' He never betrayed the secret, though he might have made his fortune by the discovery."*

After Montrose had reached the Highlands, Alaster MacColl wrote to him informing him of the arrival of the Irish force. The letter was addressed to him at Carlisle; but it fortunately came into the hands of Patrick Graham, Montrose's cousin, with whom he was in hiding. His answer to McDonnell's despatch instructed him to march immediately into Athol, where Montrose promised to meet him. The letter was dated from Carlisle, to mislead the Covenanters if it should fall into their hands. About the end of August, Alaster entered Athol, took the castle of Blair Athol, and there awaited Montrose, who soon made his appearance on foot, accompanied only by Patrick Graham. Although here in the midst of Stewarts, Grahams, Murrays, Ogilvies, and Robertsons, all royalists, the Highlanders who joined him after he had proclaimed his commission from Charles, unfurled the royal banner, and begun his march on Perth, did not nearly equal in number the Antrim regiments. Nevertheless, Montrose did not hesitate to advance through the pass of Killicrankie into the Lowlands, to encounter a much more numerous covenanting force collected at St. Johnstown (now Perth).

* Napier, p. 260.

"On the morning of August 31st, 1644, his whole forces, about 2,500, were across the Tay."*

Soon after marching, he was informed that a body of about 400 men were drawn up on a hill on his line of march, apparently to oppose his advance. They proved to be a force, commanded by Lord Kilpont, raised suddenly for the purpose of expelling the "Irishes;" but on learning that Montrose was acting under the Royal Commission they at once joined him. On reaching the plain of Tippermuir the Highlanders descried the Covenanters drawn up in battle array on the moor, about three miles from St. Johnstown, under command of Lords Elcho and Tullibardine and Sir James Scott, a brave and experienced officer. They had 400 horse on each wing and nine pieces of cannon. Montrose had three horses, but fought himself on foot, no cannon, and his little army was out-numbered by at least three to one.

"The Marquis addressed his troops in these words: 'Be sparing of your powder; we have none to throw away. Let not a musket be fired, except in the very face of the enemy. Give but a single discharge, and then at them with the claymore, in the name of God and the King.'"†

The right wing and centre were at once driven into headlong flight by Lord Kilpont and Alaster MacColl. The left wing, under Sir James Scott, fought bravely for some time, but was driven off the field by Mont-

---
\* Napier, p. 269.   † Ib. p. 271.

rose and his Athol men of the right wing, armed with the Lochaber axe. The slaughter of the pursy burgesses of Perth by the light-footed mountaineers in a flight of two or three miles was terrible, and the town was surrendered on the following day.

"Before their leader could fight another battle, a great proportion of the Athol men took at least temporary leave of him, in pursuance of their hereditary habits, and without an idea that by so doing they infringed a single rule of the military profession or lost a point in the warlike game they had so happily commenced."*

This was considered and called, very unjustly, desertion, by those who were ignorant of the conditions of service on the part of the Highlander and the regular soldier of a standing army. The privilege was perfectly understood by Montrose, who never thought of denying or punishing the exercise of it, however grieved he often was to be deprived by it of the fruits of his brilliant exploits.

"The clans," says Sir Walter Scott, "could be in no respect induced to consider themselves as regular soldiers, or to act as such. Even so late as the year 1745-6, when the Chevalier Charles Edward, by way of making an example, caused a soldier to be shot for desertion, the Highlanders who composed his army were affected as much by indignation as by fear. They could not conceive any principle of justice upon which a man's life could be taken for merely going home when it did not suit him to remain longer with the army. Such had been the uniform practice of their fathers. When

* Napier, p. 273.

a battle was over, the campaign was in their opinion ended ; if it was lost, they sought safety in their mountains; if won, they returned there to secure their booty. At other times they had their cattle to look after, and their harvests to sow or reap, without which their families would have perished for want."*

If Montrose could have been induced to propose to his Highlanders to serve under him on the conditions imposed on the common soldier, they would have replied with one voice: "My Lord Marquis, we are volunteers. The plunder we may acquire after a battle, or by a raid into the enemy's country, is our only pay. We must have liberty at all times to secure this in our mountain homes. We must be free to sow in spring and reap in harvest, to save our wives and children from starvation; and we must have the opportunity to restore the roof-tree and roof of our cottages, very likely to have been burned in the raid of some Covenanting clan, to preserve our families from death by cold within the bare walls, under the benumbing winter's blast from the mountains. In short, my lord, we must enjoy, in these and other respects, the freedom we inherit by the prescription of centuries from our forefathers; and we alone must be the judges of the sufficiency of the reasons which induce us to leave the camp. On these conditions our swords and lives are at your service. On yours, we cannot and we will not serve under your banner."

* *Legend of Montrose*, pp. 226-7. Edinburgh: 1830.

This was a fatal blow to the character of the volunteer Highlanders as soldiers, which rendered it impossible for them to form an army capable of carrying out any well-devised plan of military operations. It is a remarkable but little noticed fact that the same flaw existed in the Roman armies for more than three hundred years after the foundation of Rome, and was certainly the main cause of the slow progress made during that time in subduing the petty neighbouring states with which the Romans were continually at war. The siege of Veii was the first considerable military operation conducted with regularly paid soldiers.

In the following century the sagacity of a true statesman, Chatham, quickly perceived in what way he could avail himself of the fine military material the Highlands offered. By regular enlistment, by bounty and pay, he converted the volunteer into the regular soldier, flattering at the same time his national vanity by permitting him to retain his Highland costume. At once, the Black Watch (the Forty-twa) and other early formed Highland regiments, recruited entirely in the Highlands, became not less distinguished by bravery in battle, than by orderly, peaceable, and kindly conduct in the camp or city. Yet were these recruits, probably the wildest and most adventurous spirits of their clans, the same men who would otherwise have soon been designated in the Lowlands and

England as catherans, reivers, robbers, and thieves. They very seldom plundered any whom they did not regard as enemies. The following statement by the late Dr. Cheyne, Physician-General in Ireland, in an essay on feigned diseases among soldiers, is curiously corroborative of the high character I have given of these men :—

"In some of the cavalry regiments, in some of the Highland and other distinguished infantry battalions, in which, along with a mild but exact discipline, there is a strong attachment to the service and a remarkable *esprit de corps*, there is scarcely an instance of any of these disgraceful attempts to deceive the surgeon. . . . Among those who counterfeit disease, the Irish are the most numerous and expert; the lowland Scotsman comes next to the Irish, and what he wants in address is supplied by obstinacy. Malingering seems to me least of all the vice of the English soldier."*

The following anecdote is a contribution which I think worthy of record, in addition to the numerous acts of bravery recorded by Colonel Stuart, of Garth, in his history of the Highland regiments. A relative of mine was conversing with Sir Duncan McGregor, some ten or fifteen years ago, respecting his military experiences in the field. Few men had gone through as much active service as Sir Duncan. My friend inquired of him how often he had seen the bayonets cross in battle :—

* *Dublin Hospital Reports*, vol. iv., p. 172.

"Once," said Sir Duncan, "and once only. England had taken possession of Sicily in 1812, and a force was ordered to cross over into Italy to encounter the French, who at that time were in occupation of the country. We came in contact with the revolutionary French troops for the first time at the battle of Maida. James Macdonnel, younger brother of the Chief of Glengarry, afterwards so distinguished by his defence of Hougomont at the battle of Waterloo, and I were young officers in a Highland regiment, which was ordered to charge. At once, as if by a kind of instinct, every Highlander threw off his shoes, and then—the rush! The bayonets crossed; but, on the instant, the French turned and fled."

A large Newfoundland dog of Sir James's, for which as a child I had a tender regard, was to my grief killed in that battle.

We left Montrose in possession of Perth, where he remained three days, during which, and a few days later, his little force had been seriously diminished by the withdrawal of the Athol Highlanders and the followers of Lord Kilpont and Stewart of Ardvoirlich. Kilpont had been assassinated, under circumstances of great atrocity, by Stewart, the gloomy and half-lunatic Allan McAulay of Scott's *Legend of Montrose*. The assassin fled to Argyle, who received him with open arms, and advanced him soon after to a majority in his "pious and Godly regiment." As Argyle, with a greatly superior force, was hovering over Montrose's rear, he determined to leave the Dictator, as he called Argyle, behind, by a rapid march on Aberdeen. On his march he received some small reinforcements, the most valuable of which consisted of thirty cuirassiers, all gentlemen, under the command of Colonel Nathaniel Gordon, who had served in the wars on the Continent. Finding the bridge of Dee fortified and defended, he marched up the river to a ford, and crossing, proceeded, on the 12th of September, along the left bank of the river to within two miles of Aberdeen, and next day despatched a summons to surrender the city to the King's forces. The battle of Aberdeen was fought on this day.

"It was with a diminished force of about 2,000 followers, of whom a small proportion were cavalry, and some field-pieces taken at Tippermuir, that he again found himself in front of an enemy, not many days after he had destroyed the armament of Elcho."\*

The Aberdeen Covenanters marched out to meet the Cavaliers. They were under the command of Lord Burleigh, and were not much more numerous than their opponents—about 2,500 foot, 300 horse (in which they had a great superiority—the Royalists having about 50 horse), and some artillery. This battle was much better contested by the Covenanters than that of Tippermuir, being maintained for two or three hours; but their defeat was complete. Montrose's force was formed in great part of the Irish auxiliaries, probably two-thirds. The following extract from the diary of Sir Thomas Hope, the Lord Advocate, shows

\* Napier, p. 275.

that the statements I have made on this point were accepted in Scotland :—

"Conflict at Perth. On 1st September, 1644, being Sunday, was the conflict at Perth, where our people were mechantlie defeated by the Irish. Item; on 13th September, Aberdeen was taken by the Irish and our force defeated."

Montrose occupied Aberdeen for but one day, having received intelligence that Argyle was close upon him, with an overwhelming force, including 1,000 or 1,500 horse under the Earl of Lothian. And now, during the next two or three months, he conducted a series of masterly retreats, forced marches through the mountains, or sudden and unexpected descents upon the country of the Covenanters. He first directed his course towards the district of the eminently loyal clan Gordon, in hopes of receiving large reinforcements from them ; but the strange and disgraceful conduct of their chief, the Marquis of Huntly, and one of his sons, probably caused by jealousy of Montrose, altogether disappointed these sanguine hopes. He rid himself of his heavy baggage, buried his cannon in a morass, and retreated through the mountains into Strathspey, with the intention of crossing the Spey, and disappearing among the fastnesses of Badenoch. On arriving at the river, however, he found the opposite bank occupied by 5,000 Covenanters, and all the boats carried to that side. He was thus forced to retreat before Argyle up the

Spey, and by a long and difficult detour to reach
Badenoch, where he well knew MacCaillin More
(Argyle) would not venture to follow him. Here he
was struck down by a very serious illness, in which
his life was for some days in jeopardy. Indeed, his
death was reported among the Covenanters; and with
their usual blasphemous presumptuousness, with which
they declared their intimate knowledge of the intentions and counsels of the Almighty, some of the
zealots among their clergy announced to their flocks
that "the great God of Armies himself had slain
Montrose with his avenging hand." Notwithstanding,
he soon after presented himself again at Blair Athol.
From thence, early in October, he despatched Alaster
MacColl, with 500 of his Irishmen, on his first recruiting mission to the Western Highlands and Isles;
and he, crossing the Grampians again with his diminished force, made a rapid march, plundering the Covenanting districts on his way, to the neighbourhood of
Aberdeen. He surprised by a night march the strong
castle of Fyvie, belonging to the Earl of Dunfermline,
at this time serving in the Covenanting Scottish army
before Newcastle. Here he found himself unexpectedly within two miles of Argyle, with a greatly
superior force (2,500 infantry and more than 1,000
horse under the Earl of Lothian). Montrose had
skilfully chosen a strong position above the castle,
fortified naturally by hedges and ditches, and an

abattis of trees, felled for this purpose. For three days he was attacked by Argyle, who was uniformly repulsed, with considerable loss, but with little on the part of the besieged. Here again the great majority of Montrose's force consisted, notwithstanding the absence of Alaster and 500 of his men, of the Irish. The light-heartedness and fun of these men afforded much amusement to their graver Scottish fellow-soldiers. The defection of a company of Gordons, who, finding that Lord Lewis Gordon, son of their chief, was fighting in Argyle's army, positively refused to act against Lord Lewis, and marched away, leaving vacant the defences they had occupied, which were immediately taken possession of by the enemy, was attended with great danger. Montrose, alarmed, but assuming an air of unconcern, addressed Colonel O'Cahan, a brave officer of the Irish :—

" Come, O'Cahan, what are you about ? Take some of your hardiest men, drive those fellows from our defences, and see that we are not molested by them again. The young Hibernian replied by a rush at the assailants, for which they afterwards sought revenge by bringing him to the scaffold. In the meantime, however, he did precisely as he was directed, and drove them, horse and foot, in confusion down the hill, and his gallant company, having brought off in triumph the enemy's bags of powder, which they found in the ditches, exclaimed, with all the humour characteristic of their nation, " We must at them again, for the rogues have forgot to leave the bullets with the powder.' " *

* Napier, p. 284.

Being ill supplied with ammunition, especially ball, the Royalists, in the intervals of the assaults of the enemy, collected from all the neighbourhood every pewter vessel, dish, flagon, and utensil of still baser use, for the purpose of melting them down, and converting them into bullets. A sharpshooter among the Irish, who considered that he never missed his aim, after every discharge exclaimed, "There goes another traitor's face smashed with a —— pot."*

Montrose now resolved to take refuge once more in Badenoch, and effected his retreat with little loss, except of some Lowland gentlemen, who thought themselves unequal to bear the severity of the mountain winter. The stout old Earl of Airly and his sons, Sir Thomas and Sir David Ogilvy, refused to desert him.

Soon after his arrival in Badenoch, having learned that Argyle had sent his horse into winter quarters, and that he himself with some of his infantry were at Dunkeld, tampering with the Athol Highlanders, he resolved to attack Argyle there.

"In one night he brought his whole army four-and-twenty miles across the mountains, in the end of November, struggling through rocks and drifted snow, amidst wilds untenanted save by the eagles and deer."†

He was within sixteen miles of his opponent before he was aware of Montrose's approach. The Dictator

---

\* Napier, p. 285.   † Ib., p. 288.

fled immediately, and left his troops to shift for themselves. And now—

"At the Castle of Blair, in Athol, their original rendezvous, he was joined by his Major-General, Alaster McDonnell, who, to Montrose's great delight, brought along with him John of Moidart, Captain of the Clanranald [Macdonalds], with 500 of his sept. Alaster had been most successful in his recruiting expedition. He and the gallant Captain just named had marched together to the braes of Lochaber, where MacDonnel of Keppock [or of the Clanranald of Lochaber], the loyal chief of that country, joined them with his men [probably 300 or 400]. To these were added the Stewarts of Appin, the men of Knoidart and Glengarry [probably contributing among them at least 1,000 men], the Clan Ian of Glenco [this small sept of Macdonalds probably sending 50 or 60 men], the Laird of Glenevis, the Camerons from the western side of the Lochy, and the Farquharsons from Braemar"* [between them contributing at least 1,000 men].

Soon after, Montrose, on his march towards Inverary, was joined by a body of Macgregors and Macnabs.† And now for the first time the Highlanders, probably about 5,000 men, far outnumbered the Irish auxiliaries. Montrose was desirous to make a descent on the Lowlands, and to winter there; but the Highland chiefs prevailed upon him, in a council

* Napier, p. 289.
† I had written so far before the publication of Mr. Lecky's *History of England in the Eighteenth Century*, and have read with extreme pleasure his sketch of the sad period of my narrative. His deep research, well-considered opinions, and judicial impartiality respecting the Insurrection of 1641, afford me the highest gratification on finding so close an accordance between his conclusions and my own.

of war, to make a foray upon the Campbells, and surprise Argyle in his stronghold at Inverary. He accordingly immediately commenced, in mid-winter, a march of 120 or 150 miles from Blair Athol to Cantyre, over mountains covered with snow, and through gorges where, as he himself says, in a letter to Charles—

"I could have no guides but cow-herds, and they scarce acquainted with a place but six miles from their habitations. If I had been attacked with but 100 men in some of these passes, I must have certainly returned back, for it would have been impossible to force my way—most of the passes being so streight that three men could not march abreast."

At Lough Tay, the force divided into two bodies— one marching across the base of Ben Lawers, the other along the south-western bank of the lake; and then, as they swept through Breadalbane and Glenorchy, the country of the Campbells, they separated into three bands, one under Montrose, the second under Alaster McDonnell, and the third under John of Moidart; and each of these, breaking up into smaller bodies, spread over the country in their line of march, burning houses, driving off cattle, and shooting down men, wherever a dozen or score of Campbells gathered together to offer resistance. It is said, probably with much exaggeration, that 895 men of the Campbells were slain, and that John of Moidart and the Clanranald, with some of the men of Keppoch, on one occasion returned to the camp with 1,000 head of cattle. Argyle had no intimation of his danger till Montrose, leaving Lorne on his right hand, was marching rapidly along Loch Awe, within a few miles of Inverary. With what startled and incredulous eye and ear must the nymphs of the Awe and its Loch have seen and heard the Highland and Irish bands sweeping past, and the shrill pibrochs of the various clans echoing through the woods, having so often heard repeated the proverbial and till now truthful boast of the Campbells, proclaiming the inaccessibility of the stronghold of their chief, "It is a far cry to Loch Awe." Argyle had barely time, before Montrose was upon him, to fly from Inverary Castle, and throw himself into a fishing-boat on Loch Fine in terror, till he had lodged himself safely in the strong castle of Dumbarton.

After having burnt the town of Inverary, and ravaged Knapdale and Cantyre, Montrose turned his face northwards—"wasting Lorn even as Argyle had wasted Athol and the braes of Angus, and burnt 'the bonny house of Airly'"*—concluding the most terrible foray ever inflicted on the brave and powerful sons of Diarmid—the Clan Campbell.

Towards the middle of January, 1645, Montrose quitted Argyle's territory, and crossing the Glenmore (the great glen which runs north-east from Fort William to Inverness, in which lies the Caledonian

\* Napier, p. 291.

Canal), halted, for the purpose of refreshing the remnant of his force, near Glen Urquhart, on the north-west shore of Lough Ness, at its southern extremity. His troops were now reduced to less than 2,000 men,* nearly all his Highlanders having, as usual, gone home to secure their plunder and to prepare their little patches of arable land for the next harvest.

In the meantime, Argyle had concerted a plan for the destruction of Montrose. Argyle was to march upon him from the south with a body of his clansmen and some Lowland battalions, 3,000 strong; General Baillie, with a much greater force, was to attack him from the south-east; and Mackenzie, Earl of Seaforth, was to join them from Inverness with 5,000 men, falling upon him from the north-east; and thus, by the concentration of this overwhelming force, Montrose was to be annihilated.

In the last days of January, 1645, Argyle had just harried the Macdonnels of Keppoch, who certainly had earned small favour at his hands, and was now stationed at Inverlochy Castle, near the present Fort William. At this point of time, the bard of Macdonnel of Keppoch (Ian Lom—"Beardless John") presented himself at Montrose's camp to communicate this information.

* Napier, p. 293.

"He could scarcely give credit to this report. 'Argyle,' he exclaimed, 'dare not pursue me through Lochaber.' After a council of war, however, and finding his followers, especially his principal officer, Alaster MacDonnell, eager for the expedition, he determined to 'try back' through the mountains to the braes of Keppock and the country of Locheil."*

He resolved not to follow the direct course to Inverlochy, but taking a circuitous route over the Corryarick mountains, the braes of Keppock, and the country of the Camerons of Locheil, to pass through the domains of the Macdonells of Glengarry and Keppock, and of the Camerons, from whom he was sure of receiving numerous recruits; and hoped thus to come upon Argyle by surprise. He took with him the bard Ian Lom bound, and with the assurance that if his intelligence proved false he should be instantly shot. He lived, however, to witness from an elevated spot at the base of Ben Nevis, and to celebrate in Gaelic verse (as is said of no mean merit and poetic fire), the prowess of his clansmen in the battle of February the second. The abridged translation which I give below enables us to form some idea of the original:—

"Heard ye not! heard ye not! how that whirlwind the Gael
Through Lochaber swept down from Loch Ness to Loch Eil,
And the Campbells, to meet them in battle-array,
Like the billows came on, and were broke like their spray!
Long, long shall our war song exult in that day.

* Napier, p. 293.

"'Twas the Sabbath that rose, 'twas the Feast of St. Bride,
When the rush of the clans shook Ben Nevis's side;
I, the bard of their battles, ascended the height
Where dark Inverlochy o'ershadowed the fight,
   And I saw the Clan-Donnell resistless in might.

"Through the land of my fathers the Campbells have come,
The flames of their foray enveloped my home,
Broad Keppock in ruin is left to deplore,
And my country is waste from the hill to the shore,—
   Be it so! by St. Mary, there's comfort in store.

"Though the braes of Lochaber a desert were made,
And Glen Roy should be lost to the plough and the spade,
Though the bones of my kindred, unhonor'd, unurn'd,
Marked the desolate path where the Campbells have burn'd,
   Be it so! from that foray they never return'd.

"Fallen race of Diarmid! disloyal—untrue,
No harp in the Highlands will sorrow for you;
But the birds of Loch Eil are wheeling on high,
And the Badenoch wolves hear the Cameron's cry,—
   'Come, feast ye! come feast where the false-hearted lie!'"

A considerable part of Montrose's march lay in the line of the famous road constructed long after by General Wade, and celebrated in lofty verse by a poet, whom the "Scotch Reviewers," and I dare say "English Bards" too, with one voice pronounce to be an Hibernian, though perhaps on no better ground than Goldsmith's *Glasgow Newspaper* editor decided the nationality of Saunders MacGregor :—

"We are happy," says the editor, "to inform our readers

that Saunders MacGregor, who was hanged on Saturday last for horse-stealing, was not a Scotsman, but born at Carrickfergus, in Ireland."

"If you had seen," sings the poet, "this road before it was made,
You would lift up your hands and bless General Wade."

Let these carping critics recollect that there was no lack in those days of second-sight Highlanders who might have seen this road hundreds of years before it was made, and that it was in this sense our Hibernian intended his distich to be understood. But I fear this badinage is beneath the dignity of history.

Montrose's little army was under the necessity of dispensing with road of any kind in a most fatiguing march of two days, by which they reached the skirts of Ben Nevis early on the night of February 1st, 1645.

"Startling the herds of deer where armed men had never yet been led, they sought their way up the rugged bed of the Tarf, across the steep ridges of the awful Corryarick; now plunging into the valley of the rising Spey, now crossing the wild mountains from Glen Roy to the Spean, and staid not, until from the skirts of Ben Nevis they saw before them, under a clear frosty sky, the yet bloodless shore of Loch Eil, and the frowning towers of Inverlochy."*

Argyle soon received the alarming intelligence that Montrose was near, and posted between him and his own territory; and immediately, to the grief and

* Napier, p. 295.

shame and the silent indignation of his brave clansmen, betook himself to his galley out of musket-shot of the shore, leaving his troops under command of Sir Duncan Campbell, whom he had summoned from Carrickfergus, where he had been serving under the Earl of Leven and Monroe.

Early on the morning of Sunday, the 2nd of February, Montrose moved down to the attack. The opposing forces were nearly equal in numbers—about 3,000 each, and consisted in good measure of Highlanders.

"On the right of the royal battle was Alaster McDonnell and one regiment of the Irish; on the left, Colonel O'Cahan and another regiment of the same; Colonel James McDonnell being placed in reserve with the third. In the centre was the standard and Montrose, accompanied by a few horse, and supported by the Highlanders of Athol under the tutor of Strowan, the Stewarts of Appin, the men of Glenco, the captain of Clanranald, Keppock, Locheil, Glengarry, and Maclean. Opposed to the Royalists were the Lowland forces of Argyle placed on either wing; but his main battle and the reserve were both composed of his 'supple fellows with their plaids, targes, and dorlachs' " * [swords].

I cannot doubt that the Macdonalds and Camerons advanced to the charge to the stirring strains of the pibroch of Donald Dhu.† Byron, in his beautiful and touching description of the midnight march of the British forces from Brussels to Waterloo, gives a just

* Napier, p. 296.
† "Dark-complexioned Donald."

and true account of the powerful effect on the Highland soldier of his clan pibroch :—

"And wild and high the 'Camerons' gathering' rose!
The war-note of Locheil, which Albyn's hills
Have heard, and heard, too, have their Saxon foes—
How in the noon of night that pibroch thrills,
Savage and shrill! But with the breath which fills
Their mountain pipe, so fill the mountaineers
With the fierce native daring which instills
The stirring memory of a thousand years,
And Evan's,* Donald's,† fame rings in each clansman's ears."

The pibroch of Donald Dhu, just mentioned, was composed by a Gaelic bard in commemoration of a much greater battle, fought many years before on the same ground. The most spirited ode ever written by Sir Walter Scott is founded on the Gaelic pibroch, and presents vividly to the imagination the summons, the gathering, and onset of 10,000 Islesmen and their allies on the troops of James I. of Scotland, who were disastrously defeated :—

> "Pibroch of Donald Dhu,
> Pibroch of Donald,
> Wake thy wild voice anew,
> Summon Clan Conuil.‡
>
> . . . . . .
>
> "Come from deep glen
> And from mountain so rocky,

---

\* Sir Evan was the chief and leader of the Camerons at this battle of Inverlochy.

† Sir Donald (the "Gentle Locheil"), their chief in the Rebellion of 1745.

‡ The Clan Macdonald.

>     The war-pipe and pennon
>         Are at Inverlochy.
>     Come every hill plaid
>         And true heart that wears one,
>     Come every steel blade
>         And strong hand that bears one:
>     Leave untended the herd
>         The flock without shelter;
>     Leave the corpse uninterred,
>         The bride at the altar.
>
>             . . . . . .
>
>     "Come as the winds come,
>         When forests are rended,
>     Come as the waves come,
>         When navies are stranded.
>
>             . . . . . .
>
>     "Fast they come, fast they come;
>         See how they gather!
>     Wide waves the eagle plume *
>         Blended with heather. †
>     Cast your plaids,
>         Draw your blades,
>     Forward each man set!
>     Pibroch of Donald Dhu,
>         Now for the onset!"

After the dispersion of Donald's forces, James eagerly and perseveringly sought to get hold of him, for the purpose of inflicting condign punishment on him; and at length he was forced, to escape pursuit, to fly to Ireland, and conceal himself in his mother's (Margery

---

\* The eagle's feather indicated the rank of the individual. A single feather, a gentleman or duinewassel; two, the chief of a family; and three, the chief of a clan.

† The common heather was the badge of the Clan Macdonald.

Bysset's) territory in the Glens of Antrim. Here he prevailed upon one of the O'Neills to send a present of his head to James, which effectually put an end to all further pursuit. History has not recorded on whose shoulders the head in question had stood; but it is certain Donald Dhu had no claim to it, as, for many years after James's death, he was a noted leader of the Clandonald South.

On the present occasion, the battle was for some time stoutly fought—Highlander against Highlander, "Greek meeting Greek":—

"The brave O'Cahan had the honor of receiving the first onset, which was most manfully given by the 'flower of Diarmid.' But the three divisions of the royal army charged simultaneously, and Argyle's standard being taken, the Campbells broke in irretrievable confusion."*

The gallant Sir Duncan Campbell, Argyle's substitute, was singled out, and

" Slain by Major-General Alaster MacColl, who by one blow of a two-handed claymore swept off his head and helmet together,"†—

thus entitling himself to the *spolia opima*. Montrose's victory was complete, and the slaughter of the Clan Campbell, in a pursuit of nine miles, was terrible.

"This was the greatest disaster that ever befel the race of Diarmid, as the Campbells were called in the Highlands; it

*Napier, p. 297.
†Grant's *Memoirs of Montrose*, p. 222.

being generally remarked that they were as fortunate in the issue of their undertakings, as they were sagacious in planning, and courageous in executing them. Of the number slain, nearly 500 were dunniwassels, or gentleman claiming descent from known and respected houses. And, in the opinion of many of the clan, even this heavy loss was exceeded by the disgrace arising from the inglorious conduct of their chief, whose galley weighed anchor when the day was lost, and sailed down the lake with all the speed to which sails and oars could impel her."*

Montrose remained a few days at Inverlochy to refresh his wearied troops, and then marching in a north-easterly direction through Strath Errick, Strath Nairn, and Strath Spey, entered Elgin, the capital of Morayshire, on the 14th of February. On this occasion he had two objects in view:—(1) He was now in the vicinity of the powerful Royalist clan Gordon, and hoped to induce them loyally to join his standard. But the Marquis of Huntly, the chief of that clan, never, from jealousy of Montrose as was believed, gave him support. Lord Lewis Gordon had even fought in the ranks of his maternal uncle Argyle, and although Lords Gordon and Aboyne, Huntly's eldest and second sons, were staunch cavaliers, they were never able to bring nearly the full force of the clan to the support of Montrose. (2) The second object of this leader was to march southwards, through the eastern counties, harrying the Covenanters with fire

---

*Sir W. Scott, *Legend of Montrose*, vol. xv. of *Waverley Novels*, p. 287-8.

and sword, and hoping eventually to establish himself in the Lowlands. The fury of the General Assembly is amusingly though revoltingly exhibited at this time in their manifesto against him and his abettors. They are—

"The popish, prelatical, and malignant faction, which had displayed a banner against the Lord and his Church in all the three kingdoms, being set on fire by hell, and by the special inspiration of Satan, who is full of fury because he hath but a short time to reign. The cockatrice before hatched is now broken forth into a viper. In the meantime the hellish crew, under the conduct of the excommunicated and forfeited Earle of Montrose and of Alaster MacDonald (MacColkeitach), a Papist outlaw, doth exercise such barbarous, unnatural, horrid, and unheard-of cruelty, as is above expression."

In pursuance of this second object, Montrose, with about 3,000 foot and 300 horse, proceeded southwards early in March, meeting with no serious obstruction till he reached Brechin, soon after which he was confronted by Generals Baillie and Urrie (better known as General Hurry, a soldier of the Dugald Dalgetty class) with a greatly superior army. For two days the hostile forces occupied the opposite banks of the Isla, swollen by the melting snow and winter's rain, within musket-shot of each other. Montrose now conceived the bold project of eluding Baillie altogether, and pushing forwards into the Lowlands. At this critical moment, Lord Lewis Gordon drew off the greater number of the Gordons, "basely deserting his brother and Montrose when ready to engage the enemy." Montrose had reached Dunkeld when he learned that Baillie had defeated his object by a rapid march to Perth, and so placing himself between the royal force and the Lowlands. Thus foiled, Montrose determined to attack the rich city of Dundee with 200 horse under Lord Gordon, and 800 of Alaster MacColl's musketeers. Having sent a flag of truce by Lieutenant John Gordon to summon the city, the flag was violated by the disarming and imprisonment of Gordon; whereupon the assault was instantly ordered, Montrose superintending the attack from a hill overlooking the city. The gates were quickly burst open, their own cannon turned against the citizens, and the town plundered and fired in several places. The outrages were put, as usual, to the credit of the Irishes—

"Whether justly or unjustly," says Grant, "it is now impossible to say. In extenuation, it must be borne in mind that these brave men had no other pay or means of subsistence than what they derived from simple plunder, and moreover that every one of them that fell into the hands of the Covenanters was shot without mercy."*

In the afternoon, a breathless messenger brought intelligence that Baillie was rapidly advancing to the rescue of Dundee, that his horse were galloping down

* Grant, p. 238.

the carse of Gowrie, and would be speedily upon the plunderers. Some advised Montrose to leave them to their fate, and fly with the horse; others, that they should meet Baillie and all die fighting. "Gentlemen," said Montrose, "I implore of you to do your duty—leave the management to me, the event to God." By pipe and trumpet he summoned his soldiers, many of them intoxicated, to their colours, and, by extraordinary exertions, drew off nearly his entire force, commencing, at six o'clock in the evening of April the 4th, a rapid retreat of three days and two nights, hotly pursued by Urrie, while Baillie used every exertion, but in vain, to attack him in flank. At Aberbrothwick, which he reached before daybreak on the 5th, he took a direction at a right angle to his former course, and marching along the south side of the South Esk crossed a considerable part of Forfarshire to Kirriemuir, in the neighbourhood of which he was nearly surprised by Urrie. His officers were under the necessity of pricking with their swords some of the surbated soldiers, to rouse them to a sense of their danger and the necessity of renewing their retreat. Soon after, having crossed the South Esk, they found security from further pursuit in the defiles of Glen Esk, and among the braes of Angus and spurs of the Grampians. Montrose had now the satisfaction of learning that the force he had detached to Brechin, before the storming of Dundee, was also in safety among the mountains. His masterly retreat on this occasion rivals his most brilliant exploits in offensive war. Dr. Wishart, in his classical Latin *Memoirs of Montrose*, says:—

"I have often heard those who were esteemed the most experienced officers, not in Britain only, but in France and Germany, prefer this march to his most celebrated victories."

Whilst here recruiting his exhausted troops, many of his Highland volunteers left him for their homes, reducing his force to little more than 50 horse and 500 foot. Lord Gordon had been sent to endeavour to bring back his clansmen who had been withdrawn by his brother, Lord Lewis; and Alaster MacColl had been a second time employed to levy fresh recruits, which service he performed successfully among the neighbouring clans.

Whilst here also, James Small, a gentleman of Charles's court, disguised as a pedlar, brought letters to Montrose—one from the King, and one announcing that the Earl of Nithsdale, Lord Herries, Lord Aboyne, and thirty other Scottish Cavaliers, besieged by Major-General David Leslie in Carlisle, had broken through the besiegers, sword in hand, and were moving northwards in search of the royal army. Small, on his return to England, was captured at Edinburgh, and at once hanged for the crime of having carried letters to Montrose—one of many thousands of samples of the truculence with which the Covenanters displayed their contempt of what the purest of the elect familiarly designated as " the beggarly elements of justice and humanity."*

Montrose now determined to go in search of the gallant fugitives, and, marching through the Grampians, halted at Crieff, on the Earn, a few miles west of Perth, where Baillie was posted; who, on learning this, resolved to surprise Montrose by a night march with 2,000 infantry and 500 horse ; but the Marquis, no less vigilant than his antagonist, rode out on the same night with a reconnoitring party of his 50 horse, and, discovering Baillie's overwhelming force in the grey dawn, galloped back to his camp and ordered an immediate retreat to the wild and rugged banks of Loch Earn, ten miles west of Crieff, where he found perfect security from pursuit. Next day he marched further—to Menteith, south of Loch Katrine, where he had the satisfaction of meeting the cavaliers he was in search of, and his gallant nephew, the young Master of Napier, who had just made his escape from prison. The joy of this meeting was heightened by the intelligence that Alaster MacColl, having raised 2,000 Highlanders in his recruiting expedition, had ravaged the lands of Lord Balmerino and routed the Earl of Balcarris's regiment of horse, which had been dispatched against him; thus causing a diversion, drawing Baillie's troops away from Montrose, and leaving open

* Hume's *History of England*, vol. vii., p. 156 : Dublin, 1780.

his line of march by Athol and the Grampians to the rescue of Lord Gordon, who was now, as Montrose was informed by messengers from that lord, in extreme danger of being crushed by Urrie with greatly superior forces. Montrose at once broke up his camp, distant at least one hundred and ten miles from Lord Gordon's, and by forced marches through a very difficult country, joined him about the 1st of May, to the astonishment of Urrie, who believed him to be at this time a fugitive on the south side of the Grampians, and to the terror of the Presbyterian troops. About the same time, Alaster MacColl joined him with his recruits.

It was now Urrie's turn to retreat, which he did rapidly and skilfully, closely pursued, till he attained security and reinforcement at Inverness. While Urrie was thus reinforced at Inverness, Montrose was being weakened in the accustomed manner by the withdrawal of a large body of his Highlanders. Baillie had been burning and plundering the whole district of Athol, and the Athol men hurried home to protect their families and preserve their property. Urrie consequently again became the assailant. Montrose having taken up a position with his reduced forces (about 1,500 foot and 250 horse) at Auldern, a village a few miles from Nairn, awaited the attack of Urrie, who made a night-march from Inverness in hopes of surprising the enemy; in which he would probably have succeeded but for a singular accident. In the march across Culloden Moor and along the shore of the Moray Firth, the Covenanters had been drenched with rain, and, on approaching Auldern, fearing that the powder in their pieces had been spoiled by the rain, they went down on the beach to try to discharge them, hoping that the noise of the volley, if it occurred, would be blown out to sea. A *malignant* breeze, however, suddenly sprung up, carried the thunder to Auldern, and warned the malignant Cavaliers of the approach of the foe.

Montrose drew up his small force with consummate skill. In the village, the centre of his position, he placed some few pieces of small cannon, some banners, and pikemen, to make a show. In truth, he had no centre. On the right he placed Alaster McDonnell and his Irishes, protected from the charge of horse by the enclosures and garden-walls of the village, and favourably placed for firing on the enemy as they struggled up the rising ground, by which they had to make their attack. Here the Royal Standard was ostentatiously displayed, in the hope of attracting Urrie's principal attack to this strong position. He gave Alaster strict injunctions on no account to leave his post. On the left flank, where Montrose himself commanded, were placed the infantry of the Gordons, Camerons, and Roses, and the Gordon horse. Urrie fell into the trap prepared for him, and made his principal attack on McDonnell's strong position. Soon after the commencement of the battle, by some perfectly incomprehensible mistake, or worse, Major Drummond, an officer of Urrie's, brought his horse across the advancing infantry, causing great confusion; and Alaster, stung by the taunts of the enemy who upbraided him with cowardice for fighting from behind walls, and in disobedience of orders, rushed out to meet the Covenanters hand to hand.

The "lion-hearted" MacColl has been charged often with insubordination and rashness: but brave men are apt to be rash; and as to his inexcusable disregard of orders on this occasion, I am not aware of any other instance, in his short military career of six years, on which a charge of insubordination could be fairly founded; and he now did the best the circumstances admitted of to repair the evil effects of his rashness, by retreating to his defences, and being among the last to enter the gate through which he had made his attack. Montrose now received the alarming intelligence that McDonnell had left the inclosures, and had been routed. With the admirable presence of mind of military genius, he instantly called out to the officers of the Gordon horse:—

"'McDonnell is gaining the victory single-handed! Come, come, my Lord Gordon; shall he carry all before him and leave no laurels for the house of Huntly? Charge!'"\*

---

\* Napier, p. 332.

The impetuous charge of the Gordons that followed, drove Urrie's dragoons through his infantry and off the field, and the victory was quickly completed by the charge of the Highland foot. Some companies which had been drawn from Monroe's troops in Carrickfergus stood their ground, and perished to a man. In the fight and headlong flight, more of the Covenanters were slain than equalled Montrose's entire force. Drummond was immediately tried by court-martial, and shot. Here again, Alaster MacColl's Irishmen must have formed a large majority of the Royalist troops. In the battle of Inverlochy they about equalled the Highlanders in number.

Not many days after the battle of Auldern, Baillie having arrived with very superior forces within two miles of the camp of the Cavaliers, Montrose resolved to betake himself to the friendly fastnesses of the mountains once more. He retreated up Strath Spey, pursued by Baillie, till he approached his old refuge—the wild and rugged hills of Badenoch. Here Baillie abandoned his fruitless toil and retired to Inverness. No sooner was Montrose rid of his pursuers than he returned to the low country, for the purpose of prosecuting his raid upon the Covenanters; but on hearing that Baillie had returned to Aberdeenshire, and was wasting the Gordon country with fire and sword, he set out forthwith to the relief of his friends. On coming up with Baillie, occupying a strong position, he civilly invited the old soldier to come to even ground for a fair stand-up fight, to which Baillie curtly but very reasonably replied—"I will receive no orders from an enemy. Neither will I give battle but to please myself." The Presbyterian force was here, for the first time, inferior in number to that of the Royalists. Nevertheless, Baillie, being informed that Alaster MacColl had been sent on another recruiting mission to the Western Highlands and Isles, resolved to attack Montrose, who had taken a strong position at the village of Alford, on the Don, in Aberdeenshire, before the arrival of the expected reinforcement. On the night of July the 1st, 1645, Baillie encamped at a short distance from Alford, and early next morning moved forward to engage the enemy. Montrose, who had slept at a house two miles from his camp, joined his troops by daybreak, and gave them orders to stand to their arms, and prepare for battle.

"Unfortunately," says Grant,[*] "the Ogilvies were absent, together with Alaster MacColkeitach and Patrick (Graham) of Inchbrakie; but the Marquis had all the claymores and cavalry of the Gordon clan, whom Lord Gordon had mustered; the Islesmen and Irish; the MacDonells of Glengarry, under their chief, the valiant Angus Mac Vich Alister; the MacDonalds of Clanranald; a few of the Farquharsons under Inveray; 200 men of Strathavon, led by William Gordon of Minimore and his three gallant sons; the MacPhersons of

[* Grant, p. 260.]

Badenoch, and one or two of the lesser tribes who dwelt in the great forest of Athol. These made only 2,650 claymores, with 250 horse.

"By detachments left at various places, Baillie's force had dwindled down to 2,000 pikes and musketeers; but he had the cavalry regiments of the Earl of Balcarris and Colonel Halkett, each above 300 strong. Thus Alford was the first encounter in which the King's forces were equal or superior to the foe; so Montrose could never for a moment doubt of proving victorious."

Montrose occupied a ridge, to reach which, in coming to close quarters, Baillie had to ascend a rather steep slope exposed to the enemy's fire; and, while engaged in this movement, Balcarris made a premature charge with his whole column of horse, on Montrose's right wing. The charge was met by the Gordon horse, the Irish, and the MacDonells of Glengarry, with such firmness that the Earl's regiment retired in disorder. Balcarris rallied and brought them to the charge again and again; but at length, staggered by a volley of musketry, and charged in their turn by the Gordon horse, they turned and fled. Montrose instantly charged with his whole force, himself leading the reserve. The battle was quickly converted into a headlong rout, and Montrose's fifth victory was complete.

In the rout, nearly all Baillie's infantry perished; 1,600 of the Covenanters were counted dead on the field. One death on the Royalist side caused deep grief to Montrose and his whole army. Lord Gordon, the flower of the Scottish Cavaliers, had vowed that he would capture Baillie in the midst of his men, and had actually seized him, and was dragging him from his horse, when he received a musket-shot in the back and fell dead under his horse's hoofs. Even the Irish lamented his death. "These forrainers," says Gordon of Ruthven, "I mean the Irishes, did so incessantly bewail him, that they coeld not speak, nor call him to memorie afterwards; but did revere his obsequies with new plaintes and teares; so general was the conquest that his noble vertues and courteous cariage had made of all heartes."

Argyle and seventeen members of the "managing committee" were present at the battle of Alford. He escaped, having prudently provided for his safety before the battle, by having relays of horses ready at three different places.

Great exertions were now made by the Presbyterian parliament to raise fresh troops. A levy of 8,800 regular infantry and 500 horse was ordered. Sir John Middleton was directed to send 200 of his best dragoons from England, and Monroe was recalled from Ireland with 1,000 musketeers. Montrose also was now largely reinforced. Alaster McDonnell, after a two-months' absence, returned, bringing 700 Macleans, 500 Clanranald Macdonalds, 500 Glengarry MacDonells, and smaller numbers of other clans. These, with the Athol men brought in by Graham of Inchbrakie,

MacGregors, MacNabs, MacPhersons, Stewarts of Appin, and Farquharsons, increased Montrose's army by at least 5,000 hardy, brave, and well-armed men, and determined him to fulfil without delay his cherished purpose of carrying the war into the Lowlands.

Charles had intimated his desire and intention to force his way through the north of England and join Montrose, who consequently resolved to push on with the hope of uniting his forces with the King's at the Border. He accordingly marched by Dunkeld and Perth, where Baillie was now posted with 6,000 infantry and some hundreds of horse. Some unimportant skirmishing took place here, which scarcely interrupted Montrose's march. He crossed Kinross-shire, and passing north of Stirling, crossed the Forth at the ford of Frew, at its junction with the Teith. As he passed along the skirts of the Ochill mountains, in view of a stronghold of Argyle's, the Macleans, who had suffered many wrongs inflicted by the Clan Campbell, could not resist attacking the Castle of Gloom. They quitted the line of march, burst the gates of the Castle, and, firing it, left nothing standing but the walls, the ruins of which still form a noble object in its romantic site, a monument of clan vindictiveness.

Baillie, with 7,000 foot and 800 horse, accompanied by Argyle and the Field Committee, a band of ministers whose insolent ignorance was continually defeating the skilful tactics of the Covenanting generals, for the most part men who had acquired military experience on the Continent under Gustavus Adolphus, had closely followed the Royalists, and both the Field Committee and Montrose were anxious for an engagement. Montrose was aware that the Earl of Eglinton and other Covenanting lords of the south-west of Scotland were raising recruits; and he was eager to fight before they formed a junction with Baillie. This excellent soldier had now passed Stirling, and Montrose, having made a night march to meet him, had taken post about two miles east of Kilsyth, where Baillie, on the morning of August the 15th, unwillingly consented to attack him. Montrose had 5,000 infantry and 500 horse, Baillie at least 2,000 more.

The accounts of this battle are so confused that it is impossible to give an intelligible description of it. One thing, however, is clear—that the incredible presumption of Argyle and his church-militant clergy assured Montrose's victory before a blow was struck—by urging Baillie to fight, to which he was averse, and by repeatedly countermanding his orders and altering the dispositions he had made. The great advantage thus bestowed on the Royalists was jeopardised by a rash and premature attack made by the Macleans and MacDonalds of Clanranald, on ground where they were in imminent danger of being cut to pieces. Montrose instantly saw their perilous error, and galloping to the gallant old Earl of Airlie, exclaimed —" My Lord, you see into what a hose-net those poor fellows have fallen by their rashness! Unless relieved, they will be trodden down by the enemy's horse. The eyes and hearts of all men turn to your Lordship, and I know of none more worthy to repel the foe and bring off our comrades: forward, then, in the name of God." The brave old man, now nearly seventy years old, immediately made a furious charge on the Covenanters, seconded by Lord Aboyne and the Gordon horse; and the Highlanders, thus relieved, drove the enemy before them. The reserve brigade of three regiments of Fifeshire Whigs, whose comrades had suffered terribly at Tippermuir, deeming the day lost, fled without firing a shot. The whole Highland line now charged, and in a very short time the rout of the Covenanters was complete. They were pursued with great slaughter for many miles, 4,000 or 5,000 of them being slain. Baillie, with some of his officers and a remnant of his 7,000 escaped to Stirling; and Argyle, for the fifth time within a year, fled precipitately (as he had done at Dunkeld, Inverary, Inverlochy, and Alford) for dear life; till, reaching South Ferry and taking ship, he sailed to Berwick-on-Tweed, accompanied by some of his clerico-military friends.

Montrose was now master of the whole open country of Scotland. Outside a few fortresses the Covenanters had no force to oppose him. He was received and sumptuously entertained in Covenanting Glasgow. Glencairn and other Puritan lords of Ayrshire and the neighbouring counties fled to their brethren in Carrickfergus, and all the Whig western counties submitted to him.

## IV.

Nevertheless, the day of disaster was at hand, and in less than a month the remnant of his force remaining with him was annihilated. Still bent on his project of uniting his troops with the King's, he encamped at Bothwell Muir on the Clyde, eight or ten miles from Glasgow, and soon after moved nearer the Border in hopes of receiving reinforcements from the Homes, Kers, Douglases, and other loyal lords of the Border counties. These hopes were grievously, if not traitorously, disappointed. It is hard to believe that Stewart, Earl of Traquair, did not act traitorously While at Bothwell Muir, where forty-four years after was fought the battle of Bothwell Brig, Monmouth commanding the troops of Charles II., and where the Covenanters were addressed, as tradition says, with pithy eloquence never surpassed, as the English force advanced to the charge:—" There they're comin', and if you dinna kill them they'll kill you;" and where a friend of mine was informed by a peasant of the neighbourhood, "a famous battle had been fought, lang syne, between the Catholics and the Christians." Montrose was here joined by Sir Robert Spottiswoode, Secretary of State for Scotland, bearing a commission (for which crime he was put to death by the Covenanters) appointing the Marquis Lieutenant Governor and Captain General of the Kingdom; and here he reviewed his whole army, "and under the Royal Standard of Scotland opened his new commission, and delivered a brief but eloquent harangue, suited to the wild spirit of his hearers; and with his own good sword he knighted the flower of his Highland heroes—him of the long patronymic—Alaster Mac-Colkeitach - MhicGillespie - MhicCholla - MhicAlaster-MhicIanCattanach"*—Alexander the son of Coll the left-handed—son of Archibald—son of Coll—son of Alexander—son of Warlike John; the first and the two last chiefs of their family, the McDonnells of Isla Cantyre and the Glens, or Clan Donald South.

But now, to the grief of Montrose, at this culmination of his fame, his Highland army fell to pieces. The clans of Athole and the Macleans, 3,000 in number, hearing that their dwellings had been destroyed, and their families left to face the rigour of the coming winter homeless, departed to rebuild what the troops of Baillie in the north, and the Campbells in the west, had burned and overthrown. Others were urged by

* Grant, p. 288.

the necessity of securing their little harvests, lest if they did not their families should starve.

"Sir Alaster MacColkeitach, having unfortunately learned about this time that his friends, relations, and clansmen, who had fled from the vengeance of the Campbells to the Isles of Rachlin and Jura, were pursued thither by the Laird of Ardkinglas, the Captain of Skipness, and others acting under the orders of Argyle, became animated with a true Highland longing for reprisal; for the Covenanters treated his people with frightful severity, slaying women and children, even nurslings at the breast. All the influence of the Captain General, whom he loved so well, failed to restrain him. Every entreaty and argument were used by Montrose and by Airlie to induce him to stay, for they knew his value, and also that they never could deem themselves completely successful while the whole armed force of Scotland occupied the north of England, and could be recalled in a week. Sir Alexander replied that 'he would be no true Highlander if he preferred even the King's cause to that of his own blood and kindred'; and with 500 Highlanders and 120 chosen Irish musketeers he marched on the 3rd of September for the West country, bidding adieu to Montrose never to meet him more. . . . Filial anxiety compelled Viscount Aboyne [now Huntly's eldest surviving son] to draw off *his* followers, to save from capture and destruction his father, who was lurking in Sutherland; and on the 4th of September he also left the camp at Bothwell; but Sir Nathaniel Gordon remained."*

Thus, independently of Sir Alaster's men, about 4,000 of his Highlanders left Montrose; the Irish, with the exception of 120 men, remaining.

These Highland deserters, as they are often calum-

* Grant, pp. 290-1.

niously called, departed on an imperative call of duty, and in the exercise of their prescriptive right. Of this Montrose was perfectly aware, and though deeply grieved by their departure, never thought of forbidding or resenting it.

The further charge has often been urged against Sir Alaster, that his desertion, as it is called, was the cause of the disaster at Philiphaugh. The charge is simply absurd. It is probable that his 500 Highlanders would have gone home at this time, whether he had departed or not. I will assume, however, that he withdrew from Montrose every one of his 650 men. At Philiphaugh the Marquis had not quite 1,500 men. With the addition of MacColl's 650, his force would have numbered about 2,150. In the grey dawn of September the 13th, and shrouded in a thick mist, David Leslie fell upon him by a complete surprise with 6,000 of the flower of the horse of the Scottish army in England. It is therefore manifest that the sole consequence of the addition of Sir Alaster's men to the Royalist 1,500 would have been to have added some hundreds to the number of the slain, and perhaps fifty or sixty to that of the murdered. There is no lack, however, of responsibility for the disaster on the part of others, even of Charles himself. Leslie, as was well known, had to march from the siege of Hereford with 6,000 horse to attack Montrose, and was permitted to traverse a great part of England and Scotland entirely unmolested :—

"When Leslie was hurrying northwards, after the battle of Kilsyth, he paused at Rotherham, with men and horses so fatigued that, as he himself afterwards declared, they could have made no effectual resistance. The King was within ten miles of him, at Doncaster, at the head of 4,000 Cavaliers, while 3,000 foot, raised by the gentlemen of Yorkshire, were about to join him. He could have annihilated Leslie's force, and had not the impetuous Rupert been absent, that blow would in all probability have been struck."*

When Montrose, in obedience to Charles's orders, moved towards the Border, he expected zealous aid from the Royalist noblemen and gentlemen of that quarter, and even hoped to be joined by the King himself. He was totally disappointed in both respects. On the 4th of September he moved from Bothwell Muir with 200 horse, all gentlemen, and 700 foot. Most of the latter were Colonel O'Cahan's and Major MacLoghlin's Irish musketeers. On the 6th he received certain intelligence from Lord Erskine that Leslie was at Berwick-on-Tweed. It seems very strange that he did not instantly retreat to his strongholds among the Grampians. Passing south of Edinburgh, and descending the Vale of Gala, he was there joined by the Marquis of Douglas, with a few of the Annandale men, many of those whom his influence had induced to take arms having deserted.

"There, too, he was met by Traquair, and welcomed with warm professions of loyalty and affection; and next day there

* Napier, p. 371.

repaired to the Royal Standard a well appointed troop of horse led by John Stewart—Lord Linton—the Earl's eldest son. Traquair also undertook the duty, which he had better have left to others—that of acquainting the Marquis of the exact movements of Sir David Leslie."*

In the performance of this task Traquair most egregiously failed; and on the night of the 12th of September, when Montrose's little army of about 1,000 foot and 500 horse was encamped at Philiphaugh, Traquair sent private orders to his son to withdraw his troops, which the young noble immediately obeyed secretly, by favour of the night. In the grey dawn of the next morning, Philiphaugh being covered with a dense fog, Montrose, who had spent the night with some of his officers in Selkirk hard by, writing despatches, was alarmed by the sound of musketry, and instantly seizing his rapier, mounted the first horse he found, and galloped across the Ettrick to the camp, followed by his officers. They soon perceived the hopelessness of the contest, and at first thought merely of selling their lives as dearly as possible, but were persuaded by Sir John Dalziel, of Glenae, to take advantage of their immediate assailants being diverted by the plunder of the baggage, and to cut their way by dint of sword through the enemy. The proposal was adopted; and Montrose, followed by Lords Douglas, Crawford, Napier, and Erskine, and some

* Grant, p. 293.

other gentlemen, fled at full speed up the Yarrow. It is remarkable that Sir John Dalziel was brother of the Earl of Carnwath, the person who took Charles out of the field after the loss of the battle of Naseby, seizing hold of his horse's bridle, and saying, " Will ye go upon your death ?"

The main body of the Irish retired to an enclosure on an eminence, " which," says Guthry, " they maintained till Stuart, the adjutant, being among them, procured quarter for them from David Leslie, whereupon they delivered up their arms, and came forth to a plain field, as they were directed." The clergy, however, argued that it would be impious to spare the lives of such wretches, that Stuart alone had been admitted to quarter, and that the rest should be put to death, quoting in support of their outrage on "the beggarly elements of justice and humanity":—"Now go smite Amalek, and utterly destroy all that they have, and spare them not, but slay both man and woman, infant and suckling, ox and sheep, camel and ass."

In my opinion, it matters not at all whether the quarter was intended to include the Irish or not. What followed was in either case an atrocious massacre: 400 of these brave men were on the next morning marched two miles up the Yarrow, enclosed in the courtyard of Lord Cassilis's Castle of Newark, and shot down to a man. The 150 Irish who accompanied Sir Alaster met the same fate in May, 1646, in Cantyre ; 300 women were slain in the camp, and says Grant :—

"Eighty other women and children, fugitives from that dreadful scene, were overtaken at Linlithgow by the Covenanters, who flung them over a high bridge into the foaming Avon, fifty feet below ; there they were all drowned, for a few who reached the banks were thrust back by pikes and destroyed. Thus man and woman, infant and suckling, perished; for again and again were the conquerors told that the curses which befel those who spared the enemies of God would fall upon him who suffered one Amalekite to escape."*

Montrose effected his escape to the Highlands, and during the winter and spring of 1646 used every exertion, with little success, to raise another Royalist army, till Charles wrote him orders from Newcastle on the 19th of May, 1646, to lay down his arms, and retire into France.

Sir Alexander McDonnell, having succeeded in raising 1,200 Highlanders, had been engaged in warfare with the Campbells during the winter ; and now Sir David Leslie marched into the Western Highlands to attack him with four regiments of infantry, three troops of horse, and three of dragoons, reinforced by Argyle with a body of his clan burning for revenge. On 25th of May a sanguinary battle was fought in Cantyre, where it borders on Knapdale :—

"Sir Alaster, with his native Islesmen, his 150 musketeers,

* Grant, p. 301.

and the clan MacDougal, an ancient tribe of Lorne, endeavoured to defend Tarbet, part of his old and lawful patrimony, from which his father had been expelled by the Campbells [and James the Sixth in 1615]. The whole day the strife continued among the mountains, and, armed only with their swords and shields, again and again the Celtic warriors flung themselves upon the serried pikes of the Covenant, and many acts of high individual valour were performed. By nightfall the contest was ended, but Sir Alaster was completely routed, with the loss of 200 men, eight pieces of cannon, and all his ammunition. By a stratagem he retired to his boats, and sought shelter in the Isles, leaving a garrison of 300 MacDougals and Irishmen in the Castle of Dunaverty,"* on the coast of Cantyre, two or three miles from the Mull—an old castle of the MacDonalds, in which the Lord of the Isles received and sheltered Robert Bruce at the time when his fortunes were at the lowest.

Leslie besieged the castle, and the garrison were soon compelled to surrender for want of water. They were butchered to a man; the Rev. John Neaves, Leslie's Chaplain, threatening him with all "the curses which befel Saul for sparing the Amalekites," if he spared the men of Dunaverty.

"Thus urged, 260 gallant soldiers were hurried into eternity; while Argyle and the sanctimonious ruffian, Neaves, walked together among the falling corpses, literally ankle-deep in blood. 'Now, Master John,' said the godly Marquis, turning with a sardonic grin to the preacher, 'for once you have got your fill of blood.'"†

More than fifty years ago I saw the bones of some

---

\* Grant, p. 331-2.   † Ib. p. 332-3.

of these noble fellows bleached white in the sands of the sea-beach below the headland on which the old castle stood. And thus perished, by a dastardly and inhuman massacre, the last of Sir Alaster MacColl's heroic Irishmen (the Montrose Irish Brigade) in less than two years after leaving their native shores. His own short but brilliant career was now also approaching its end. To escape the vengeance of Argyle, he fled to Ireland about the same time that Montrose became an exile in obedience to Charles's commands. In less than a year and a-half after his return to Ireland he was killed at the battle of Knock-na-noss ("the Hill of Fawns"), near Kanturk, in the County Cork, on the 13th of November, 1647.

The narrative I have just given of Sir Alaster's proceedings in the end of 1645 and beginning of 1646 conclusively disposes of the last charge preferred against him—viz., that he at this time betrayed Montrose, and refused to rejoin him in his present distress. MacColl could not by possibility have rendered him more valuable and efficient support than by occupying Argyle's forces in the West Highlands, and drawing away Leslie to Cantyre, the extreme west, while Montrose was zealously but vainly endeavouring to raise an army among the Gordons and other Royalists of Aberdeenshire and the neighbouring eastern counties.

The following account of Sir Alaster's death is quoted from the lamented and accomplished Miss

Annie Hutton's admirable translation of the confidential correspondence of Rinuccini with the Court of Rome, during his residence in Ireland as Papal Nuncio :—

"The two hostile armies approached each other on the 13th November, 1647. The Catholic army consisted of 6,000 infantry and 1,200 horse, and the English of 5,000 foot and 1,300 horse, under the command of Baron Inchiquin, while our forces were led by Viscount Taaffe, with General Alexander Macdonnell of Ulster as his lieutenant. The Catholics were drawn up in the following manner. In front of the right wing was MacDonnell with 3,000 infantry, composed of Ulster and Connaught men, and the Irish Islanders [viz., Highlanders], supported by Colonel Purcell, with two regiments of cavalry. On the left wing was Lord Taaffe, with nine Munster legions, to the number of 4,000 infantry and two regiments of horse. In this order the battle was begun. Inchiquin [the leader of the Parliamentarian army] had placed the best part of his troops opposite to Macdonnell, whom he greatly feared, and not without reason, as his soldiers, after firing one or two volleys, threw away the musket, and, seizing the sword, rushed upon the enemy with such fury that they pursued for three miles, killing them as they fled to the number of 2,000, without losing more than five men, after which they took cannon, carts, and baggage, of which they retained possession for a whole hour. Meantime, on the other wing the one regiment commanded by Lord Castleconnel fired but one volley, and then, with all the Munster troops, fled in the most disgraceful manner, throwing away their arms in their flight; and, though the General cut down some of the cowards with his own hand, he was unable to keep them back! Hence the cavalry also of the right wing, which, under Purcell, had made their way bravely, on hearing and seeing the flight of the infantry, abandoned their colonel, and fled. Their flight was so ignominious and so rapid that Lord Inchiquin, after pursuing them a short way and killing many, returned, and, with the rest of his army, charged the victorious Catholic party, who, believing that the victory was on their side, and were standing carelessly around the enemy's cannon, when suddenly attacked could only defend themselves in a disorderly manner, and fell to the number of 700. After a great slaughter of the enemy 3,000 escaped, but with the loss of the cannon they had just captured. General Alexander Macdonnell, who had separated himself a little from his troops to see after a messenger whom he had sent with an account of his proceedings to the other wing, met, on his return, fourteen of the enemy's horse; refusing quarter, he killed four of them, and, while parleying with their captain, was treacherously stabbed from behind by a soldier, and at once fell dead."

He is still remembered in the south of Ireland by a very singular piece of music composed in his honour, and remarkably expressive of "all the currents of a heady fight." It was published by Mr. Bunting in his last collection of Irish Melodies, under the title of "McDonnell's March." His fame still lives in the Highlands of Scotland also :—

"The memory of this great warrior is still revered in the land of the Gael, where the peasants still sing, 'Oran do dh' Alasdhair MacColla,' a song which was composed in his honour by a female harper, Dorothea of Luing, when she saw his galley, with the broad banner of Macdonald displayed, sailing through the sound of Luing towards Ireland, the land of his exile."*

* Grant, p. 333.

## V.

Up to June, 1642, the aid contributed by England and Scotland to the distressed Protestants of Ulster consisted of 1,500 men sent by Charles in November, 1641, and 2,500 under Monroe, in April, 1642, an instalment of the 10,000 promised by Scotland; and between them the service they had performed consisted in the recovery of Newry and the raising of the siege of Coleraine; and yet, unaided, the Ulster Protestants in arms had now reduced the rebels to despair.

"Monroe," says the Rev. Dr. Leland (*History of Ireland*, book 5, chap. 5, p. 176-7), " with an appearance of amity and respect, visited the Earl [Lord Antrim] at his castle of Dunluce; was hospitably received; but at the conclusion of an entertainment, gave the signal to his followers. The Earl was made prisoner, his castle seized, and all his houses committed to the custody of the Scottish forces."

This is Carte's disputed narrative :—

" Two months wasted in total inaction or the most frivolous enterprises, revived the spirit of the rebels, recalled them from their retreats, and enabled them once more to collect their forces. The charge of opposing them now devolved on the English forces of Ulster [that is, the English and Scotch settlers], for the Scots [viz., Monroe's soldiers] were totally employed in ravaging the adjacent districts, and exporting vast herds of cattle into Scotland. Sir Phelim O'Nial appeared once more at the head of an army, but was bravely encountered by Sir Robert and Sir William Stewart, two

English commanders. After a sharper action than had hitherto been fought in Ulster, the rebels were driven to flight with the loss of 500 slain, many wounded, and a number of prisoners. [This was the battle of Glenmaquin, already mentioned.] It was proposed to prosecute this advantage, but the English were distressed and necessitous, and Monroe refused his assistance."

Dr. Leland continues :—

"This apparent horror of putting too speedy a conclusion to the war must immediately have been attended with the most pernicious consequences, had not the rebels been dispirited by ill success, and in want of every necessary for the prosecution of their enterprise. Such was their dejection, that when Monroe, in the month of July, at length showed some disposition to proceed more vigorously, the Irish Chieftains held their council, and resolved to abandon a cause rendered utterly hopeless by repeated defeats and disappointments, and to fly to foreign countries from the rage of their victorious enemy."

I desire to call especial attention to this perfectly true account of the state of the struggle between the Catholics and Protestants in Ulster in less than eight months from the commencement of the civil war. In less than six months after it the Irish were disgracefully foiled at the siege of Drogheda; and Dundalk, Carlingford, Newry, and Armagh, which had been taken by them, were recovered from them; and in almost every encounter with the Protestants in Ulster they had been defeated with such extreme disproportion of loss of life on their part as would have been not only disgraceful, but unintelligible, if they had been armed as their antagonists were. Bearing in mind that the Ulster Protestants had as yet received no external aid whatever, I hold this condition of things to be perfectly inconsistent, not only with the preposterous exaggerations of Clarendon and Temple, but with any very considerable loss of life among the Ulster Protestants capable of bearing arms.

This complete defeat of the insurgents was effected by the posthumous valour of the 150,000 Protestants massacred by Sir John Temple. Mr. Froude, indeed, says:*—" The English Parliament being occupied with fighting the King, the Scots sent a force (England providing the money) which gradually drove the rebels out of Ulster." This is either gross ignorance or gross misrepresentation. The strange inactivity of the Scotch troops in Ulster is one of the most difficult to comprehend and remarkable incidents of the war. I can imagine no explanation of it but that it was adopted in concert with the like conduct on the part of Parsons and Borlace. It admits of no doubt that a policy of nursing the rebellion was pursued by them at first for the purpose of improving the harvest of confiscations which they hoped by and by to reap for themselves and their friends.

Monroe arrived at Carrickfergus about the middle of April, 1642, with 2,500 men. He immediately recovered Newry from the rebels, and, marching

* *English in Ireland*, vol. i., p. 115.

northwards, raised the siege of Coleraine, meeting no resistance in either case. Except some vigorous cattle-lifting, he may be said to have hibernated thereafter till 1646, when he was disastrously defeated by Owen Roe O'Neill in the battle of Benburb. If he had acted with energy on his arrival in Ireland—joining his troops to the Ulster Protestant force under Sir R. and W. Stewart, the insurrection in the north would have been stamped out at once; and very probably Owen O'Neill would have declined to enlist in a cause the utter defeat of which he would have learned from his expatriated kinsmen.

In August, 1642, Alexander Leslie, Earl of Leven, who had served with great distinction under Gustavus Adolphus, arrived in Carrickfergus with a reinforcement of 7,500 men. Leslie outdid Monroe. He marched into Tyrone, and, rivalling the French king who "marched up the hill, and then—marched down again," returned to Carrickfergus, and soon after to Scotland, having first truly predicted for Monroe the fate that awaited him at Benburb four years later. The conduct of Leslie and Monroe, and the tardy and feeble efforts made by England and Scotland at this time to avenge the slaughter of such a multitude of their countrymen, induce me to entertain a suspicion that the Puritan leaders did not give credit to Temple's fabulous history. There is no doubt that the people of England accepted it literally.

A graphic account of an incident not very creditable to England, at a time when the Protestants were to the Roman Catholics in that kingdom as forty to one,* is given by the Rev. Joseph Lister, a Dissenting minister in Yorkshire :—

"About this time did the rebellion in Ireland break out, and many thousand Protestants, of all ages, sexes, and degrees, were put to death with great inhumanity and cruelty; and great fear come upon the Protestants in England, those villains giving out, that what they had done there was by the King's commission, and that in a little time the English Protestants (or heretics, as they called them) should drink of the same cup; and it was verily believed by many that it would be so, if God should suffer it; and oh, what fears and tears, cries and prayers, night and day, was there then in many places, and in my dear mother's house in particular! I was then about twelve or thirteen years of age, and though I was afraid to be killed, yet was I weary of so much fasting and praying, and longed to see those days and nights over. I remember one public fast day (for godly ministers appointed many, and kept them in their respective places),—Mr. Wales kept many at Pudsey; it was two miles from Bradford, and thither my pious mother and all the family went constantly upon those days; I have known that holy Mr. Wales spend six or seven hours in praying and preaching, and rarely go out of the pulpit; but sometimes he would intermit for one quarter of an hour, while a few verses of a psalm were sung, and then pray and preach again; and oh! what confession of sin did he make! what prayers, tears, and wrestling with God was in that place in these days! What tears and groans were to be seen and heard in that chapel! I am sure it was a place of weepers. But that day, I say, which I am speak-

---

* Hume's *History of England*, vol. vi., p. 392.

ing of, I think about three o'clock in the afternoon, a certain man that I remember well (his name was John Sugden) came and stood up in the chapel door, and cried out with a lamentable voice :—'Friend,' said he, 'we are all as good as dead men, for the Irish rebels are coming; they are come as far as Rochdale, and Littlebrough, and the Balings, and will be at Halifax and Bradford shortly.' He came, he said, out of pity and good will, to give us notice. And having given this alarm, away he ran towards Bradford again, where the same report was spread about. Upon which the congregation was all in confusion; some ran out, others wept, others fell to talking to friends, and the Irish massacre being but lately acted, and all circumstances put together, the people's hearts failed with fear; so that the Rev. Mr. Wales desired the congregation to compose themselves as well as they could, while he put himself and them into the hands of Almighty God by prayer: and so he did, and so dismissed us. But oh! what a sad and sorrowful going home had we that evening, for we must needs go to Bradford, and knew not but incarnate devils and death would be there before us, and meet us there. What sad and strange conjectures, or rather conclusions, will surprise and fear make! Methinks I shall never forget this time. Well, we got home, and found friends and neighbours in our case, and expecting the cut-throats coming. But at last some few horsemen were prevailed with to go to Halifax, to know how the case stood. They went with a great deal of fear, but found matters better when they came there, it proving only to be some Protestants that were escaping out of Ireland for their lives into England; and this news we received with great joy."

After six months' higgling between the English and Scottish Parliaments, 2,500 men, under Robert Monroe, were landed at Carrickfergus, in April, 1642, to avenge the wholesale slaughter of their fellow-countrymen; and five months later, Lord Leven landed at the same place with 7,500 more, making up the 10,000 that Scotland had undertaken to furnish. Elizabeth had sent 20,000 to subdue the rebel Earl of Tyrone; and a little before this time, England and Scotland confronted one another on the banks of the Tweed, with about 50,000 men, in a religious quarrel involving no question of doctrine considered by either party necessary to salvation—but matters relating to the government of the church, and the colour, shape, etc., of the garments in which the clergy should officiate.* The Long Parliament enlisted 4,000 recruits for Lord Essex's army in London alone in one day.†

Monroe arrived at Carrickfergus on the 15th of April, 1642, and set out on the 27th for the recovery of Newry. The resistance offered to him on the way was quite contemptible. At Kilwarlin Woods, near Banbridge, he says he killed 152 men with a loss to himself of two men. It follows that the Irish fought,

* "The grievances which tended" says Hume (*History of England*, vol. vi., p. 389) "chiefly to inflame the Parliament and nation, especially the latter, were the surplice, the rails placed about the altar, the bows exacted on approaching it, the Liturgy, the breach of the Sabbath, embroidered copes, lawn sleeves, the use of the ring in marriage, and of the cross in baptism. On account of these were both parties contented to throw the government into such violent convulsions; and to the disgrace of that age and this island, it must be acknowledged that the disorders in Scotland entirely, and those in England mostly, proceeded from so mean and contemptible an origin."

† Hume, vol. vi., p. 490.

as indeed Colonel Sir James Turner informs us they did, "with half-pikes, swords, and daggers, which they call skeens," against muskets. The Rev. Mr. Clogy also, who was living among the rebels in Cavan, states, when relating the failure of the plan to seize the Castle of Dublin, in which arms and ammunition to a great amount had been collected :—

"All their strength and hope lay in the surprisal of this place, without which they had neither arms for horse or foot, nor ammunition. For in the Earl of Strafford's time, no man in Ireland of whatsoever degree could have above 10lbs. weight of powder at once, and that out of the Castle, by order in writing."*

On the 1st of May, Monroe took an island in Loughbrickland. "On the way there," says Monroe, "some prisoners taken were hanged thereafter," and the whole sixty taken in the island "were put to the sword, and our prisoners, which they had, released." Newry was taken with little trouble. Sir James Turner, an eye-witness, speaking of the prisoners taken in the castle, says :—

"Most of them, with many merchands and tradesmen of the towne, who had not been in the castle, were carried to the bridge and butchered to death—some by shooting, some by hanging, and some by drowning, without any legal processe. Lord Conway was the principal actor. Our sojors thought they might do as much anywhere else, and so runne upon 150 women or thereby, who had got together in a

* *Memoirs*, p. 170.

place below the bridge, whom they resolved to massacre by killing and drowning. Just at that time was I speaking with Monroe; but seeing afare off what a game these godless rogues intended to play, I got a horseback and galloped to them with my pistol in my hand; but before I got at them they had despatched about a dozen; the rest I saved."

Soon after, Monroe, having left a garrison in Newry, returned to Carrickfergus, and, after raising the siege of Coleraine, took up the trade of cattle-lifting, which he prosecuted with distinguished success, while the Plantation Protestants were reducing the rebels to despair. At this critical time the spirits of the insurgents were revived, and a resolution was formed to renew the struggle, in consequence of the arrival of Owen Roe O'Neill at Castle Doe, in the north of Donegal, with a considerable supply of arms and ammunition, and 100 trained Irish officers drawn from the armies of France and Spain. A force was immediately despatched to escort him to Charlemont. Sir Phelim O'Neill was superseded, and Owen Roe was unanimously chosen as their leader, and the representative of the chiefs of his name, the ancient Princes of Ulster.

"Owen O'Neill was an officer who had seen much active service on the Continent, and, in addition to his experience as a soldier, he possessed in an eminent degree that discernment and foresight that enabled him to see the errors of the past, and to prepare for the future. While he did everything to raise the spirit of the insurgents, he not only spoke strongly in detestation of their previous barbarities and excesses, but he took all opportunities of disgracing and punishing those who had taken a prominent part in them. He is even said to have burnt the houses of some who were notoriously guilty, and to have declared openly that he would rather join with the English than suffer such wretches to escape punishment."*

He had lately acquired high fame by his defence of Arras, besieged by 34,000 French troops, and was certainly a brave, cautious, and skilful soldier; but he unfortunately attached himself to the faction of the Papal Nuncio Rinuccini, who by his ignorance and incredible presumption, even in disregard of his instructions from the Court of Rome, largely contributed by his mischievous proceedings to the result of this war, so disastrous to the Roman Catholics. Immediately on conclusion of the truce in 1646, between Ormond and the Roman Catholic Confederates, he declared violently against it—assumed, in fact, the political and military management of the affairs of Ireland into his own hands, upset the government established by the Kilkenny Confederates, and ordered Owen O'Neill to march to Kilkenny to support him. Instead of being sent back to his Archbishopric of Fermo at an hour's notice, he was zealously supported by the Celtic Irish, and obeyed by Owen O'Neill.

This leader had just given a crushing defeat to the Parliamentarians under Monroe at Benburb, near Armagh. Monroe, whose forces had been much diminished by detachments he had been obliged to

* Wright's *History of Ireland*, book v., chap. vi., p. 709.

send to Scotland to check the alarming progress of Montrose in that country, marched from Carrickfergus with about 5,000 men to attack O'Neill at the head of about an equal force. Monroe's army was almost annihilated, and O'Neill's victory had the immediate effect of swelling his army from 5,000 to 10,000 men. He had the fairest prospect, if he had been allowed to follow up his success, of driving the Scottish Puritan army out of Ireland.

On hearing of these insane proceedings, with what pious exultation must Cromwell have exclaimed—"The Lord has delivered them into my hand!"

I rejoice that the object with which I write does not require me to enter into the particulars of the history of this war. It affords a glaring example of the political fatuity which, times without number, brought disaster on the Celtic Irish in their contests with or rebellions against the English. I have quoted already the proverb that "Experience keeps a dear school, but fools will learn at no other;" but I maintain that he is no fool who *does* learn at that school. Dame Experience has taught the Irish by a thousand examples that political success imperatively demands steady political union; but they have not learned the lesson to this day. The Home Rulers are already split into hostile factions.

In the beginning of the Civil War of 1641 in Ireland there were four well-marked parties. (1) The Parliamentarians, viz.—the Scottish Puritan forces under Leslie and Monroe, and their allies, the Ulster Protestants; (2) The Protestant loyalists under Ormond; (3) The Anglo-Irish Roman Catholic Lords of the Pale; (4) The Celtic-Irish Roman Catholics. By far the weakest of these four parties in the commencement of the war was the Puritan faction. By a steady union among the other three parties in support of Charles I., in which they could all have concurred, they could easily and certainly have crushed the Puritans, and driven Monroe out of Ireland. But they could never cordially unite; and as the war proceeds it becomes day by day plainer that the gradually increasing strength and dogged determination of the Parliamentarians, and the insane dissensions among the other three parties, must inevitably end in the triumph of the first, and the utter ruin of the rest. With what cruelty that ruin was inflicted may be learned by the perusal of Mr. Prendergast's able and touching history of the Cromwellian settlement. What would have been thought in England and Scotland, if, on the conclusion of the civil war, every Cavalier who had not exhibited "constant good will" towards the Parliament, and who possessed an acre of land, had been driven to the mountains of Wales or the Grampians—some, the true-hearted Royalists, to starve: others, in proportion to the mildness of their malignancy, being reprised with mountain land for a portion of the rich acres for the loss of which they were deemed to be entitled to compensation ? Such, however, was the terrible award inflicted upon the wretched landholders of Ireland.

I have already stated that in the beginning of the Civil War of 1641 there were many murders committed by the Irish in Ulster (including those who died from exposure to the weather without food and clothing), and even some massacres of a few defenceless persons here and there by terrified and vindictive mobs; but I altogether deny that there was anything remotely approaching a general massacre such as is described by Clarendon and Temple. I neither excuse nor palliate the murder or massacre of women, children, or old men, no matter when, where, or by whom perpetrated. They are utterly inexcusable, and equally abhorrent to natural humanity and Christian principle. But there are degrees in inexcusableness; and I assert, roundly and without qualification, that the English barbarities of this kind perpetrated in Ireland were much greater, more cruel, and more inexcusable than those for which the Irish were responsible. The murders and massacres by the Irish were almost always, as I have said, pepetrated by mobs, and the Roman Catholic gentry and the Kilkenny provisional government uniformly exerted themselves to prevent them; whereas the English murders and massacres were usually perpetrated by the organized forces of the Government, or even by direct order of the Government itself or its officers, as when Ormond was commissioned by Parsons and Borlace to drive the rebels from a station a few miles from Dublin, his orders were "to burn and destroy their haunts, and to kill all the inhabitants capable of bearing arms," and when (as we are informed by Dr. Borlace, whose history of these transactions was written in defence of his near relative the Lord Justice) Sir W. Cole's regiment killed 2,500 rebels in battle, but besides "starved and famished of the vulgar sort, 7,000."

And here let me warn my Saxon brethren of England, and my "brither Scots," that it will not redound to their credit for comparative humanity to contrast their murders and massacres in Ireland with those perpetrated by the Irish upon them. I would gladly have avoided this subject, but Mr. Froude's slanders compel me to expose his ignorance and carelessness. While he and almost every Protestant historian who treats of this period continue to quote and credit Temple's slanders, I will not consent to listen in silence—"I will not undergo their sneaps without reply." I could easily set out a terrible array of Saxon atrocities in Ireland; but I will here mention only two massacres, which I produce not only on account of their magnitude, but because I believe the reader will be startled by their being quoted as at all belonging to the category of massacre. I allude to the war for the extermination of the elder branch of the FitzGeralds in Munster, and Mountjoy's war against Hugh O'Neill in Ulster, both in the latter days of Elizabeth. I have already recounted the horrors of these wars on the authority of Englishmen, eye-witnesses of what they record. "Absurd!" I think I hear Mr. Froude exclaim; "these were legitimate wars, prosecuted against notorious and ungrateful rebels." I offer no objection to the slaughter of any number of rebels in the field. That is all fair; but I insist that all the women, children, and old men who were starved to death as the necessary and deliberately intended result of the manner in which these wars were carried on, *were massacred*, and that in a far more cruel way than if the victim had been despatched in the way proposed by another savage :—

> "Batter his scull, or paunch him with a stake,
> Or cut his weasand with a knife."

I have witnessed, in our miserable days of famine, death by starvation, and know well how infinitely the sudden death by sword or knife is preferable to the lingering torture of death by famine. The gush of blood that follows the stroke of the sword, or the spattered brain, shocks and revolts; but it requires little reflection to conclude how beyond measure more dreadful to the sufferer is the lingering death. The number of victims, too, must have come near the fabulous number (Temple's 150,000) slain in the first two months of the rebellion by the Ulster Celts of 1641. The cattle of the peasantry were driven to the camp, food of every kind was carried off, or, if it could not be carried off, was burnt, and the standing crops reaped, the sword (by what our English critics, with a sneer in the sleeve, would describe as a practical Irish bull) being turned into the reaping-hook. The soldiers were sent into the fields with orders to cut off the ears of the growing crops with their swords. Let any reader who doubts the truth of what I have just written, revert to what I have related respecting these wars on the authority of the Poet Spencer, and Fynes Moryson, the private Secretary of Mountjoy, and of Mountjoy himself.

"The horrid accounts," says Dr. Leland,* " of famine and distress in those parts of Ireland most exposed to the calamities of war, can scarcely be suspected of falsehood or exaggeration, when we consider the effects of these civil commotions in the very city of Dublin. I have seen an account of the rates of provisions sold in Dublin in the year 1602 [towards the end of Mountjoy's war], authenticated by the signature of John Tirrell, Mayor, by which it appears that 'wheat had risen from 36 shillings to £9 the quarter; barley malt, from 10 shillings to 43 shillings the barrel; oat malt, from 5 shillings to 22 shillings the barrel; pease, from 5 shillings to 40 shillings the peck; oats, from 3 shillings and 4 pence to 20 shillings the barrel; beef, from 26 shillings and 8 pence to 8

* *History of Ireland*, vol. ii., p. 442.

pounds the carcase; mutton, from 3 shillings to 26 shillings the carcase; veal, from 10 shillings to 29 shillings the carcase; a lamb, from 12 pence to 6 shillings; a pork, from 8 pence to 30 shillings."

Between 1604 and 1641 three men occupied, to the calamity of Ireland, the post of chief governor of the country—Chichester, Strafford, and Parsons. I need not say more than I have said above respecting the two last. Sir Arthur Chichester was Lord Deputy for eleven years. His virtues may be seen recorded as somewhat superhuman on his tomb in Carrickfergus Church; and it is true that his rule was far less pernicious to Ireland than Strafford's or Parsons'. He gives an account, however, of a military expedition he made from Carrickfergus to Dungannon, on which, he himself relates that, as he marched along Lough Neagh, he killed every living thing he met; and he deliberately recommends the starvation of the people as preferable to fire and sword, which work too slowly for the purpose of extirpating the Irish enemy.

Within a year of the outbreak of the war, a legislative and governing body was established at Kilkenny, which conducted its affairs, the circumstances considered, with surprising wisdom and moderation. A meeting of the Roman Catholic clergy at Kells was soon followed by a General Synod held at Kilkenny, which was joined by the Roman Catholic nobility of the town and neighbourhood, and such others as came to Kilkenny to aid in the formation of a government for the country. One of their first acts was the framing of a deed of association, afterwards adopted by "The General Assembly of the Confederate Catholics of Ireland," of which the following is a copy :—

"I, A.B., do in the presence of Almighty God, and all the saints and angels in heaven, promise, vow, swear, and protest to maintain and defend, as far as I may, with my life, power, and estate, the public and free exercise of the true Roman Catholic religion, against all persons that shall oppose the same. I further swear that I will bear faith and allegiance to our sovereign lord King Charles, his heirs and successors; and that I will defend him and them, as far as I may, with my life, power, and estate, against all such persons as shall attempt anything against their royal persons, honors, estates, and dignities; and against all such as shall directly or indirectly endeavour to suppress their royal prerogatives, or do any act or acts contrary to the regal government; as also the power and privileges of parliament, the lawful rights and privileges of the subjects, and every person that makes this vow, oath, and protestation, in whatever he shall do in the lawful pursuance of the same. And to my power, as far as I may, I will oppose, and by all ways and means endeavour to bring to condign punishment, even to the loss of life, liberty, and estate, all such as shall either by force, practice, councells, plots, conspiracies, or otherwise, attempt anything to the contrary of any article, clause, or anything in this present vow, oath, or protestation, contained. So help me God."*

Mr. Froude and numerous other writers assert that the Irish, above everything else, sought at this time to shake off their connection with England. Nothing

* Borlase: *History of the Irish Rebellion*, fol. 74.

can be wider of the truth, till near the end of the war,
when they were brought to the verge of utter ruin by
Cromwell; then, indeed, they were willing, in their
despair, to have recourse to any saviour who could
stand between them and impending destruction. Let
the reader learn from Mr. Prendergast's *Cromwellian
Settlement* what reason the prostrated Irish Roman
Catholics had to dread that destruction. The uniform
language of the Irish towards Charles, for the first
eight or nine years of the war, was that of subjects
devotedly loyal. The Puritans of the Long Parliament,
indeed, often rivalled them in professions; but these
were shameful and false lip-homage. The Irish confirmed the truth of their professions to a King who
had cruelly wronged them. At the time of the cessation of hostilities in 1643, the Catholic Confederates
presented £30,000 to Charles, a large sum considering
their poverty—half of which, because of their poverty,
they stipulated should be contributed in cattle. The
truce enabled Ormond to send over to Chester 3,500
men in aid of the King; and at the same time Inchiquin sent over some regiments under Lord Dungarvan,
which took part in the siege of Gloucester.[*]

In August, 1644, they provided vessels to transport
2,000 men to join Montrose in the Highlands of Scotland. The men had been raised, indeed, and equipped
by Lord Antrim; but the Confederate government

---

[*] Wright's *History of Ireland*, vol. ii., pp. 1, 2.

approved of the important aid intended for the royal cause, and the transports were furnished by them.

Again, at the time of the peace in 1646, the Catholic Confederates undertook to send into England 10,000 men under the Earl of Glamorgan, in support of Charles; but which, owing to circumstances over which they had no control, were not sent. They engaged to send 6,000 men by the 1st of April, and 4,000 more by the 1st of May. But on the 5th of that month Charles surrendered himself to the Scots, with whom he remained a prisoner till they sold him to similar imprisonment to the Parliament—in which condition he remained, with the exception of a few hours after his escape from Hampton Court, till his fetters were struck off by the hand of death. After his surrender to the Scots all aid from Ireland was impossible.

The Nuncio Rinuccini, a witness above suspicion in this matter, writing in cipher to Cardinal Pamphili, says :—

"Your Eminence will see that the first clause of the oath taken in this Assembly is fealty to the King, and this all the bishops took without hesitation. This point is so warmly insisted upon by everyone, the clergy included, that a Nuncio could not in any wise oppose it without giving rise to a suspicion that his object here was not simply that of his embassy; which the ill-affected have frequently, even without this reason, insinuated in my case. Therefore I took care from the first in nowise to oppose their professions of loyalty, and as I found the proposal still pending for sending 10,000 soldiers to the King, I put in a few words to urge them to do so; saying that they should uphold and assist the King, prove themselves good subjects," etc.*

Language of perfectly similar import is frequently used by the Nuncio in his confidential communications to the court of Rome in earlier letters.

The supreme governing and legislative body was constituted on the model of the British Parliament. There was a sort of House of Lords, and a House of Commons elected by the towns and counties, by whom an executive was created, consisting of twenty-four members appointed by the legislative body, and styled the Supreme Council of the Confederate Catholics of Ireland. Persons were appointed in the counties like justices of the peace, to decide minor cases, from whom an appeal lay to bodies constituted for similar purposes, empowered to deal with more important cases for the provinces, and from whom an appeal lay to the Supreme Council. Till its vitals were disordered and disorganised by the insane dissensions of the various factions, the proceedings of this Parliament will compare favourably with those of any other assembly convened under similar circumstances.

"They began," says Cooke Taylor, "with sanctioning the war which had been undertaken 'against sectaries and Puritans, for the defence of the Catholic religion, the prerogative of the King, the honour and safety of the Queen and royal issue, the preservation of the rights and liberties of Irishmen,

* *The Embassy in Ireland of Monsignor G. B. Rinuccini*: Miss Annie Hutton's translation, p. 259.

and the lives and fortunes of the Confederates,' as just and necessary. They declare that no order of the King, whom they very properly regarded as an unwilling instrument in the hands of their enemies, should be obeyed, until they were certified by their own agents of his real intentions. They directed that an oath of association should be taken by all the members of the confederacy, and that no distinction should be made between the Old and New Irish. They denounce the heaviest censures of the church on those who remain neutral in the contest; and prohibit, under pain of excommunication, any injury to a Protestant who was not an adversary to their cause. They direct that exact registers should be kept of all murders and cruelties committed by the Puritans, in the several provinces, but prohibit retaliation under the severest penalties. They ordain that provincial assemblies, composed of laity and clergy, should be formed for local government, but that the chief authority should be lodged with a national council, to which the others should be subordinate. There were some other regulations of minor importance; but the above articles contain the substance of the ordinances published by the Catholic clergy; and we can discover in them no trace of the bigotry and persecuting spirit vulgarly attributed to that much-calumniated body."\*

Soon after the truce agreed upon by Ormond and the Confederate Catholics in 1643, two deputations waited upon Charles in Oxford—one representing the views and demands of the Confederates, the other those of the Protestants of Dublin. The contrast between the requirements of the two deputations is both curious and instructive. The Catholics claimed the freedom of their religion, and the repeal of the Penal Laws, the

---

\* *Civil Wars of Ireland*, vol. i., p. 286. Edinburgh: 1831.

summoning of a free parliament, and the suspension of Poynings's Law, seminaries for the education of Roman Catholic priests and lawyers, an act of amnesty in favour of the insurgents, and the reversal of their attainders, exclusion from the Irish Parliament of all who did not reside in the country and did not possess Irish estates, an Act declaring the independence of the Irish Parliament, and that no chief governor should hold his office for more than three years (during which time he should be incapable of acquiring new lands in the country), inquiry by Parliament into all breaches of quarter and inhuman acts committed by any party, and exclusion of all persons guilty of such crimes from the amnesty, and their punishment in due course of law. All the important items of these demands have been conceded by the free action of the enlightened Imperial Parliaments of modern times.

The Protestant deputation, on the other hand, demanded—

"The rigorous execution of all penal statutes against recusants; the immediate and total disarming of Catholics; the compelling them to repair all damages sustained by Protestants; the punishment of all offences committed by recusants, without pardon or mitigation; the vesting of all estates forfeited under the administration of Parsons, in the Crown; and after satisfaction had been made to such as claimed under the Acts of Parliament, the distribution of the residue entirely to British planters."*

* Cooke Taylor, vol. i., p. 294.

"Previously, a parliament consisting almost entirely of partisans of Parsons and Borlace had in 1642 resolved upon new Penal Laws, as well as enforcing the old ones with the utmost rigor, and talked with a puritanical hatred of Popery."*

Dr. Reid, in his *History of the Presbyterian Church in Ireland*, gives in extenso a petition from the Ulster Presbyterians setting forth under thirty-one heads the grievances they suffer from the Catholics. One of these is both ludicrous and melancholy:—

"13. In many places of the land where Protestants are forbidden and restrained [I have never heard on any other authority of any such], Papists are permitted to keep schools; to some whereof such multitudes of children and young men do resort, that they may be esteemed rather universities, teaching therein not only the tongues, but likewise the liberal arts and sciences."

Assuredly "the force" of insolence and bigotry "can no further go" than this.

Thus it is plain that the Confederate Catholics were contending for exemption from intolerable grievances; and the Protestants, not only for the perpetuation of the oppression of their countrymen, but for its aggravation by new Penal Laws. In short, in this war the Roman Catholics fought to recover their liberties and property, and to secure their religion; the Puritans to confirm and extend the tyranny inflicted on Ireland by centuries of misgovernment, and brought to perfection by Strafford.

* Wright's *History of Ireland*, vol. i., p. 718.

The sentiment has often found expression in England,—"How happy would it have been for England if Ireland could have been sunk in the Atlantic for twenty-four hours!" Too true. But alas! alas! how greatly more happy for Ireland itself would that fate have been from 1172 to 1829! For six hundred and fifty years of cruel and unwise misgovernment, "*L'empire des Anglais en Irlande, depuis leur invasion de ce pays en 1169, jusqu' à la fin du siècle dernier* [1800] *n'a été qu'une tyrannie.*"\* This severe denunciation is the conclusion to which every impartial Englishman, Scotsman, and Irish Protestant, and every foreigner, without exception, who studies Irish history, will come. Speaking of De Beaumont's history, Mr. Lecky says :—

"For the whole subject of the Penal Laws, I would refer to the most admirable 'Introduction Historique' to the work of Gustave De Beaumont, *L'Irlande, Sociale, Politique, et Religieuse.* Very few writers have ever studied Irish history so accurately and so minutely as M. De Beaumont, and he has brought to it the impartiality of a foreigner, and the political insight and skill which might be expected from the intimate friend and the faithful disciple of De Tocqueville."†

\* Gustave de Beaumont: *L'Irlande, Sociale, Politique, et Religieuse*, 5th edition. Paris 1842, vol. i., p. 15.

† Lecky : *England in the Eighteenth Century*, vol i., p. 296, note i.

## VI.

Several events occurred in 1646 which contributed to hasten the termination of the war so ruinous to the Irish Roman Catholics. The peace between Ormond and the Kilkenny Confederates was concluded in March; Charles surrendered himself to the Scots in May. The troops sent into Ireland by Scotland, and paid by England, were disastrously defeated by Owen Roe O'Neill at Benburb, and Rinuccini, encouraged by this great victory and Owen Roe's subservience to him, took the reins of government into his own hands. This presumptuous Italian had been about six months in the country, and was consequently profoundly ignorant in regard to the policy and measures necessary to be adopted to promote its true interests, to unite its various factions against the common enemy, and to disentangle its perplexed and tangled affairs.

"Never had Ireland presented so miserable a scene of inextricable confusion as at this moment. At least four independent governments had established a footing on its soil, and were contending for sovereignty over the whole. The Parliamentarians were strong in the north and south; the Earl of Ormond ruled in Dublin, the Supreme Council at Kilkenny, and the Papal Nuncio at Waterford."*

Such being the condition of affairs, Rinuccini, by a solemn decree, signed in his own name, appointed a

* Wright, vol. i., p. 48.

new council for the government of the kingdom. He was himself president, who in fact exercised sovereign authority in all affairs of government, and his councillors were the Archbishop of Cashel, three bishops, and eight laymen, of whom the Earl of Glamorgan, as blind a bigot as himself, was one. In these proceedings he received hearty support from the Celtic Irish.

Immediately after the battle of Benburb, when, if O'Neill had followed up his victory, he could with certainty have driven the remnant of the Scottish troops out of Ireland, he marched his whole force to Kilkenny, by orders of the Nuncio, to support him against Ormond and the Confederates.

"The friars and monks had, from the very commencement, been devoted to the cause of the Nuncio, and they preached everywhere that the calamities which afflicted them arose from the neglect of his advice, and the little regard shewn to the interests of their holy religion. One of these incendiaries had even the audacity to seize the colours of a regiment that was marching by orders of the general, and to denounce damnation against all who proceeded further. The officers remonstrated indignantly, but the superstitious soldiers threw down their arms and dispersed. The regular clergy by no means joined in these excesses, but they found on this, as on other occasions, that the mob is more easily led by the fanatics of the several monastic orders than by their own parochial ministers."*

From the date of the peace in 1646, to the end of the war, by the surrender of Galway on the 12th of

* Cooke Taylor, vol. ii., p. 42.

May, 1652, the Parliamentarians had no more valuable and efficient allies than Rinuccini, and after his departure from Ireland in February, 1649, the Roman Catholic Bishops who succeeded to his office and adopted a policy little less ruinous than his. The troops, too, of the various factions afforded powerful aid to the Parliamentarians by their insane dissensions, continually thwarting and opposing one another, and often being on the point of meeting each other in actual conflict. Their idiotic dissensions were equivalent to an army of Irish volunteers in aid of the Parliament. During the whole of this period the Irish were almost uniformly defeated by the Puritans. The only very remarkable exception to this disgraceful truth occurred at the siege of Clonmel by Cromwell himself, where, as also at the siege of Kilkenny, he learned that his atrocious policy of massacre at Drogheda and Wexford was not so successful as he expected it would be.

Clonmel was defended by Hugh O'Neill and some 1,500 of Owen Roe's Ulster soldiers. Hugh was the last of a series of four very remarkable and able men, who played an important part in the history of their country from the reign of Elizabeth to the time of this siege. Cromwell had just taken the city of Kilkenny, having granted the garrison honourable terms of surrender. He complimented them on the gallant defence they had made, and declared that but for the treachery of the civic authorities, he would have raised the siege. At Clonmel O'Neill made a heroic defence, till his last charge of powder was spent; and he then withdrew the remnant of his soldiers unobserved, by night. The siege was undertaken early in April, 1650, and a practicable breach having been quickly made, the assault was ordered.

"The first attempt to storm was defeated with so much slaughter that the infantry refused to advance a second time; and Cromwell was forced to appeal to the cavalry. Lieutenant Henry Langley and several other officers of horse gallantly volunteered; the private troopers followed the example of their officers, and a second storming party was formed under the command of Colonel Culin. The second assault was so fierce that the Irish were driven from the breach; but O'Neill had by this time built a new wall at the head of the street which the breach faced, and lined the adjacent houses with musketeers. The assailants were unable to overcome this new obstacle. Culin and several others fell. Langley's left hand was cut off by a blow of a scythe, and the greater part of the detachment was either killed or wounded. In these two assaults Cromwell lost more than 2,000 of his best soldiers. He would not venture on a third; but changed the siege into a blockade, and determined to wait the slow effects of famine."*

These two examples afford evidence that the terror excited by the massacres of Drogheda and Wexford, which is put forward in miserable palliation of those savage atrocities, did not quite answer by its success Cromwell's anticipations. Upon the whole, however,

* Cooke Taylor, vol. ii., p. 38.

the conduct of the Irish during this period affords a most disgraceful exemplification of the proverb—

"Quem Deus vult perdere, prius dementat."

If any trading Irish patriot, who has not yet entered the *rat*-trap, disputes the truth of what I have here just written, with pain and shame, I pledge myself to produce chapter and verse in proof of every statement I have made.

It may be safely assumed that the civil war would, at all events, have ended in the certain victory of the Long Parliament, having regard to the overwhelming superiority of force of England and Scotland, and the necessary division in Ireland between the Covenanting Presbyterians of Ulster and the other three Irish parties; but if these had presented a firmly united front to the enemy, and conducted the war with mutual trust, bravery, and such leadership as Montrose gave his Irish brigade, the peace that would have closed the war would have been very different indeed from the inhuman barbarity of the Cromwellian Settlement.

VII.

I now gladly return to the proper object of my essay. I again request the special attention of the reader to the following facts. In July, 1638, Archbishop Laud writes to Strafford :—

"The Scottish business is extream ill indeed, but what will become of it God knows, but certainly no good, and his Majesty hath been notoriously betrayed by some of them. There is a speech here, that they have sent to know the number of Scotchmen in Ulster; and that privately there hath been a list taken of such as are able to bear arms, and that they are found to be above 40 thousand in Ulster only. This is a very private report, and perhaps false, but in such a time as this I could not think it fit to conceal it from your lordship, coming very casually to my ears."

This estimate, of course very loose, was made three years before the massacre of 1641. In 1657, Major Morgan, Member of Parliament for the County of Wicklow, in a debate respecting the lands of the Lords Clandeboy and Ards in the County of Down, stated that "in the north the Scotch keep up an interest in garb and all formalities, and are able to raise 40,000 fighting men at any time." These statements (though of course far from accurate, together with the fact, always to be borne carefully in mind when speculating upon the Protestant population of Ulster after 1641, viz., that there has never been any pretence at a second Plantation of Ulster after the supposed extermination of the men, women, and children of the first), are utterly inconsistent with anything remotely approaching to truth in the allegations of Clarendon and Temple. Clarendon himself, in his short view of the state of Ireland, says:—" The Scots in Ulster were very numerous and possessed considerable towns in 1648."*

The excellent Dr. Oliver Plunket, Roman Catholic Archbishop of Armagh, judicially murdered in 1681, writes to Rome in 1673 as follows :—

"In the diocese of Down and Connor, as also in many other dioceses, there is a large number of Presbyterians (who are especially numerous in Ulster), of Anabaptists, and Quakers, and hence these dioceses [viz., Roman Catholic] are exceedingly poor. And it must here be remarked, that the Presbyterians, who are an offshoot of Protestantism, are more numerous than Catholics and Protestants [viz., Protestants of the Established Church] together."

If Temple's calumny were true, Ulster ought to have been by far the most Roman Catholic province of Ireland. It is, however, and has ever been since the Plantation of Ulster, certainly by far the most Protestant. It is believed that till the famine of 1846-7, which fell more heavily on the Roman Catholics than on the Protestants, the former, in spite of the Penal Laws, had been gaining on the latter. Dr. Bourke, Roman Catholic Bishop of Ossory, in his *Hibernia Dominicana* (Brussels, 1762), gives the following account of the relative numbers of Protestants and Roman Catholics in each province :—

* Clarendon's *Rebellion*, vol. viii., p. 83.

| Nomina Provinciarum. | Numerus Protestantium. | Numerus Papistarum. |
|---|---|---|
| Conacia (Connaught), | 21,604 | 221,780 |
| Lagenia (Leinster), | 203,087 | 447,916 |
| Momomia (Munster), | 115,130 | 482,044 |
| Ultonia (Ulster), | 360,630 | 158,028 |
| The Four Provinces, | 894,851 | 1,309,768 |

This also must be a rough estimate, at least so far as the Protestant population is concerned. Such as it is, however, it gives much the greatest comparative Protestant population to Ulster. The following enumeration from the Irish Census for 1861 may be received as pretty near the truth :—

| | Ulster. | Connaught. | Leinster. | Munster. |
|---|---|---|---|---|
| Protestants of the Established Church, | 391,315 | 40,595 | 180,587 | 80,860 |
| Presbyterians, | 503,845 | 3,088 | 12,355 | 4,013 |
| Protestants of other persuasions, | 52,473 | 3,429 | 12,140 | 8,609 |
| Jews, | 52 | 1 | 338 | 2 |
| Roman Catholics, | 966,613 | 886,023 | 1,252,553 | 1,420,076 |
| Total, | 1,914,298 | 933,136 | 1,457,973 | 1,513,560 |

From these figures we conclude that in 1861 the per centage of Protestants to Roman Catholics was :—

14·13 to 85·9 in Leinster;
6·20 „ 93·8 „ Munster;
5·18 „ 94·8 „ Connaught;
49.50 „ 50·5 „ Ulster.

Thus in Ulster Protestants and Roman Catholics were nearly in equal numbers; in all the other provinces the Roman Catholics were far more numerous than all sects of Protestants together.

During a great part of last century à tourist in Ulster would have found everywhere in the mountains and bogs, the Celtic race, the Irish language, and the Roman Catholic religion; and the arable land occupied by men of English or Scotch blood, speaking English or Scotch, and Protestants. Since then the Celts have been slowly mixing with the Saxons, attracted especially to towns where any manufacture was taking root. The Curate of Belfast in the end of last century assured an old friend of mine that when he settled in Belfast there were not in that town and the neighbouring parish of Shankhill five Roman Catholic families; there are now in the town upwards of 55,500 Roman Catholics.

Immediately after the conclusion of the war a commission was appointed to make inquiry respecting the murders that had been committed during the rebellion. The commissioners were officers of Cromwell's army—Puritans, perhaps not over-exigent in regard to the amount and kind of evidence sufficient for the conviction of a Papist. They, in fact, held court-martials. Mr. Froude says :—

"The remnant of the Ulster murderers who had survived the wars remained to be brought to late justice. A high court of justice, under General Fleetwood, was held at Kilkenny, in the hall of the Assembly, to try them. Sir Phelim O'Neill and 200 others were convicted and executed. All the rest had been consumed in a war, the waste of life in which, compared with the population of the country exposed to its ravages, stands unparalleled in the annals of mankind."*

I hope Mr. Froude, when he wrote this, was ignorant of the facts of the case. If not, this passage is a marvel of scandalous disingenuousness. How many of these two hundred and one murderers does the reader suppose were Ulster murderers—murderers of the Ulster massacre? Just one—not one hundred, gentle reader, but the unit one—viz., Sir Phelim O'Neill. The remaining two hundred were murderers of Leinster, Munster, and Connaught, where there has never been the pretence of a general massacre in this war. This strange but certain fact gives strong corroboration to the belief that Temple's account of the Ulster massacre is an outrageous exaggeration. We have all heard of the Temple of Truth; here we have the Temple of Falsehood. Mr. Froude must excuse me if I assure him, with perfect truth, that the spirit who dictates such garbled and calumnious histories as Temple's and his,

* *English in Ireland*, vol. i., pp. 128-9.

of this most deplorable epoch of Irish history, as little resembles Thalia, the muse of faithful, truthful, and impartial history, as the strumpet resembles the honoured and chaste Roman matron—

> "Chaste as the icicle
> That's curdled by the frost from purest snow,
> And hangs on Dian's temple."

## VIII.

I have now, in conclusion, to invite my reader to witness, under the guidance of the Rev. Mr. Clogy, Rector of Cavan, the proceedings of the insurgents in the County Cavan, one of the six forfeited counties, during the first eight months of the war, throughout which he resided near the centre of the county and in the midst of the rebels. His testimony is given in his most interesting life of his stepfather-in-law, Bishop Bedell, a prelate of rare and truly apostolic virtues, never surpassed, if even equalled, by those of any other bishop of the Episcopal Protestant Church of Ireland, except Bishop Berkeley—

> "Manners with candour are to Benson given:
> To Berkeley, ev'ry virtue under heaven."—*Pope*.

Bedell had procured the translation into the Irish language, and the publication at his own expense, of the Old Testament, and by his zealous but gentle and tolerant advocacy of the Protestant faith, was by far the most dangerous opponent the Roman Catholic priesthood had ever encountered in Ireland. He had even made a convert of the brother of the Roman Catholic Bishop of his diocese of Kilmore. In proof that the Rev. Mr. Clogy is free from all taint of partizanship in favour of Roman Catholics, I quote the following fiery and shocking denunciation of them. He has just given a copy of a Latin letter of Bedell to the Roman Catholic Bishop of Kilmore, on which he remarks :—

"Did ever Polycarpus of Smyrna, or Ignatius of Antioch, or any other of the famous bishops and martyrs of the Primitive Church, who had their Father's name written on their foreheads—*i.e.*, that made an open confession of the faith of Christ crucified, come nearer to him who before Pontius Pilate witnessed a good confession, and show a greater contempt of the world, and of death itself, under the cruel persecution of the pagans, than this our magnanimous confessor and blessed martyr of Jesus declareth in this short and pithy epistle, under the cruelty of bloody Papists? whose hatred of, and cruelty of all sorts against the people of God doth as far exceed that of their elder brother, the pagan, as they may find one day (if God be true) that the torments of hell, and those everlasting burnings prepared for dogs, and sorcerers, and whoremongers, and murderers, and idolaters, and for whosoever loveth and maketh a lie (for Popery is nothing else but a great and presumptuous lie against the true God and the truth of God contained in the Scriptures of truth, and every particular of it), are above those of their Popish purgatory; and they that follow him that was a murderer from the beginning, and abode not in the truth, may justly expect to be ranged with him, and to suffer as murderers, unless they repent of the works of their hands;

that worship devils and idols of gold, and silver, and brass, and stone, and wood, which neither can see, nor hear, nor walk; and of their murders, of their sorceries, and of their fornications, and of their thefts, *nec turba deorum talis ut est hodie.*"

Speaking in general terms of the beginning of the outbreak, Mr. Clogy describes the atrocities in terms quite as strong as any other of the Protestant authorities; but it is remarkable that from beginning to end of his memoir he does not mention one case of murder witnessed by himself or any person on whose truthfulness he could rely. This, indeed, affords only negative evidence; but it is surely passing strange, if an average of 1,800 murders weekly during the first two months of the war (Temple's average) were being perpetrated in this county, that no mention should be made of them. One of the most noted massacres was said to have been perpetrated at Belturbet, within about ten miles of Cavan, of which he makes no mention, but the accredited account of which mixes up the only too probably true evidence as to the murders, with a miracle, palpably false, that the bodies of the slain came floating up the river against the stream some days after the massacre, to testify their abhorrence of the chief author of the massacre, who was standing on the bridge of Belturbet.

"After a mass," says Mr. Clogy, "that bloody and unparalleled massacre commenced. And here I confess my frailty.

I am at a stand, like a man astonished, and like a man that wine hath overcome; how to write or express anything of it, that is beyond all expression (that was written in such large bloody characters in one instant, *tanquam signo dato*, through all parts of the kingdom of Ireland) without tears of blood, or a *quis talia fando*, or *quis cladem illius noctis (ubiq' luctus ubiq' gemitus, et plurima mortis imago)*; or rather with Jeremiah, *quis dabit capiti meo lymphas, et oculis meis fontem aquarum, ut defleam noctes atq' dies confossos filios populi mei*. . . . One day's warning might have saved thousands of lives of poor innocents that knew not the right hand from the left. That bloody harlot, the mistress of witchcraft, was so drunk with the blood of saints, and with the blood of the martyrs of Jesus, that she made no discovery of the design, as Delilah did often to Sampson ere he lost his hair, but surprised us (while our watchmen and sentinels were buried in sleep and security, or wrangling together and sadly falling out upon the main guard) with swift destruction, by rapine, fire, and sword, without the sound of a trumpet or the alarms of war; destruction was cried, for the whole land was spoiled: suddenly were our tents spoiled, and our curtains in a moment! . . . There were no people under heaven lived in a more flourishing state and condition for peace and plenty of all things desirable in this life, when on a sudden we were turned out of house and hold, and stript of all outward enjoyments, and left naked and bare in the winter, and on the Sabbath day put to flight that had no place to flee to for refuge. The land that a little before was like the Garden of Eden was speedily turned into a desolate wilderness. *Horresco referens quod animus meminisse horret luctuq' refugit.* We soon forgat prosperity when we fell into the hands of brutish men and skilful to destroy. O! the multitude of cries that went up to heaven that are joined with the loud cries of the souls under the altar.\*—Rev. vi., 9, 10."

\* *Memoir by the Rev. Alexander Clogy, of Life of Bishop Bedell.* London, 1862, pp. 159-61.

This vague declamatory denunciation does not inspire confidence that it is free from exaggeration, or that the picture it presents is a copy from nature. The naked truth required no exaggeration to create both horror and pity. No doubt there were numerous murders—perhaps some isolated massacres of some dozens of English or Scotch by savages prompted by "man's inhumanity to man," and urged by hatred and revenge; but at all events there was a multitude of refugees from every corner of the forfeited counties, of whom the great majority, the women and children, could have had no complicity in the crime which led to their calamity, and who were now reduced in a moment from a condition of comfort and affluence to the last extremity of destitution, without raiment to defend them against the wintry elements, and without food to sustain them for the three or four days necessary to enable them to reach the nearest city of refuge. The barbarity of the Irish who drove them out under such circumstances admits of no excuse, and they are justly responsible for every death that occurred in consequence of it before the fugitives reached their friends. Even then their sufferings were not over. Thousands perished after this by disease generated by the miseries they had undergone, and want—the result of the most disgraceful and criminal failure of England and Scotland to furnish prompt and liberal support to the victims of their own cruel policy of wholesale spoliation.

There were probably few of the Ulster planters into whose thoughts it ever entered that they were not justly and legitimately possessed of the lands assigned to them by James. The spoliation of the Irish of the forfeited counties was the crime of James and the two nations, who heartily approved of the robbery, which was at once to establish civility in a fourth part of Ireland : England and Scotland were therefore bound, in honor and conscience, to stand between the expelled planters and the ruin brought upon them by the consequences of the national sin. Their case was very similar to that of the West Indian slave-holders, who had been encouraged by successive governments, and by public approval, in reducing to slavery such multitudes of their fellow-creatures. Queen Elizabeth was one of the earliest English slave-traders; having chartered on her own account, for that infamous traffic, the *Jesus of Lubec*. Queen Anne's government, in the treaty of peace of Utrecht, as the fruit of all Marlborough's victories, demanded and received the monopoly of the slave-trade. The noble and unparalleled act of generosity and justice by which the nation acknowledged and expiated the national sin, and saved from ruin the slave-holders, their accomplices, will be recorded in history and redound to the signal honour of the Empire to the end of time. In 1641 the national conscience was in deep sleep, and the wretched fugitives, so far from being compensated for their terrible losses, were not even provided by the state with the means of present support, and of transport to England or Scotland from the ports to which they had fled.

Let us now turn to the testimony of the Rev. Mr. Clogy as to what he witnessed with his own eyes during the first eight months of the rebellion. He testifies that the rebels, as has been already mentioned, were unprovided with arms, and did not murder during the first mouth after the outbreak, thus contradicting himself :—

"All their strength and hope lay in the surprisal of this place [the Castle of Dublin, where arms and ammunition for 10,000 men were in store], without which they had neither arms for horse or foot, nor ammunition. For in the Earl of Strafford's time no man in Ireland of whatsoever degree could have above ten pounds weight of powder at once, and that out of the Castle, by order in writing. . . . And for a whole month's time, or thereabouts, they meddled not with the Scots, though they had driven out all the English that were in the fields or in unwalled villages; they had no resting place; as thinking too hazardous to engage two such potent nations at once, till they had first dispacht one."*

Mr. Clogy's account of the treatment Bishop Bedell received from the insurgents is equally honourable to them and to that most excellent man, and is in strange

* Clogy, pp. 170, 173.

contrast with the merciless treatment of Roman Catholic ecclesiastics when they fell into the hands of the Puritans. "They never," says Cooke Taylor, "spared a priest;" and certain it is they very seldom did so. A revolting instance of their barbarity occurred a few years after this time.

The Roman Catholic Bishop of Ross had been taken prisoner by Lord Broghill, a nobleman of somewhat loose political principles, who had lately been enlisted by Cromwell himself in the parliamentary ranks. Broghill was in London on his way to join Charles II. at Breda, when, to his astonishment, he was visited by a messenger from Cromwell, who was desirous, the messenger said, to know when his Lordship could receive him. Broghill, in reply, said there certainly must be some mistake with regard to him; but on receiving the most positive assurance that there could be none, he desired the messenger to inform Cromwell that he would wait upon him immediately. Cromwell, however, presented himself at Broghill's lodgings before he had time to get ready for his proposed visit. Cromwell informed him that the Council were well acquainted with his proceedings, and were about to order his arrest, but, at Cromwell's urgent request, held back their order, to afford him an opportunity of reasoning with his lordship respecting his intention of joining Charles. The result of the interview was that Broghill returned to Ireland a strenuous supporter of the Parliament. He had just given a severe defeat to the Irish at the time of the above-mentioned capture of the Roman Catholic Bishop of Ross. Near the field was a strong castle held by the Irish. Broghill requested the Bishop to persuade the garrison to surrender, promising him his life if he succeeded. He was conveyed to the castle, and summoning the defenders, exhorted them by their duty to God, their religion, and their country, to hold out to the last extremity against the enemy. The ecclesiastical Regulus was brought back to the camp, and forthwith ordered by Broghill to be hanged. The " ferocious piety " of the Puritans, as some one has happily called it, which dictated this outrage, was as disgraceful to the Protestants as the contrasted humanity of the insurgents in their treatment of Bishop Bedell was creditable to them.

As Cromwell piously attributes the glory of the Drogheda massacre to God, Mr. Clogy is careful to attribute the mercy of the rebels to the compulsion exercised over them by an overruling Providence.

"And indeed," says he, "God was a little sanctuary to him, and caused the enemy to entreat him well in the day of his calamity, and the desolation of God's people; for the Lord protected him, and his family, and children, and servants, from all personal violence; and did so still the enemy and avenger, that none was ever suffered to do his person any harm, or to touch any of his for their hurt: he was *mediis tranquillus in undis*, as Noah in his ark; as if that of the Apostle had been immediately spoken to them : ' And who is he that will harm you, if ye be followers of that which is good?' Or as if the slaughter-master had given special order concerning him, as Nebuchadnezzar, the Chaldean destroyer, did to Nebuzaradan concerning Jeremiah in like case. . . . The rebels told him he should be the last Englishman they would put out of Ireland. He was the only Englishman in all the County Cavan that was permitted to stay in his own roof. There was but little spare room in his castle, which was no way fencible against the least violent assault, and the poor stript people, that had a plenty of all earthly accommodation but a little before, were now content to lodge in the outbuildings, in the church, or church-yard, in heaps of straw or hay, and to feed upon boiled wheat or whatever the enemy had left, that could not so suddenly consume so great plenty as was everywhere to be found."*

And here the Bishop, his sons, and Mr. Clogy, with the crowd of fugitives who had put themselves under his protection, remained unmolested by the insurgents till the 18th of December. In the meantime Bedell had drawn up a remonstrance for the rebels to be laid before the Lords Justices, setting forth their grievances, and promising to lay down their arms on receiving redress of them. If Parsons and Borlase, and their brethren in iniquity in Dublin, had been desirous of putting an end to the rebellion, this remonstrance would have been eagerly received with favour; but their object was not "to seek peace and ensue it," but to nurse the rebellion with a view to confiscations, and their answer accordingly attained this object. About this time the insurgents requested the Bishop to

* Clogy, pp. 179, 180, 181.

dismiss the fugitives under his protection; and on his refusal to do so—

"At last they resolved upon another speedy and inhuman course, and tell him that though they loved and honoured him above all the English that ever came into Ireland (because he had never done wrong to any, but good to many), yet they had received strict orders from their Council of State at Kilkenny (which was the metropolis of the rebels), that if he would not put away the distressed people from him they must immediately, without any more ado, take him away from them."*

Accordingly they carry him, his sons, and Alexander Clogy, prisoners to a castle on an island in Lough Erne, the ruins of which are still standing, about two miles from the Bishop's palace, Loughouter Castle, in which a few years after Owen Roe O'Neill died, when on his way to encounter Cromwell. Here Bedell was kept a prisoner till 7th January, 1642.

"The young men were put in irons lest they should surprise the fort at any time, for sometimes they would all be drunk, and sometimes but one keeper left to look after six prisoners. But God gave them such favour in the eyes of the keeper of the prison (as Joseph of old) that he abated much of the rigorous commands that were given him, and did ease them of their irons, and gave them leave to use divine exercises of God's worship, as to pray, read, preach, and sing songs of Zion in a strange land, as the three children, though in the next room the priest was exercising his Babylonish mass."†

* Clogy, p. 204.   † Ib., p. 207.

On the 7th of the next month they were set at liberty by an exchange of prisoners. Sir James Craig and Sir Francis Hamilton, leaders of the Scots in Cavan, had fortified themselves in two castles about a mile distant from one another, and two miles from Loughoughter Castle. A garrison of Scots and English was formed in the castles, and huts and cabins erected about them, covered with cow-hides. Here, after remaining unmolested for a month or six weeks, they were besieged by the rebels :—

"Whereupon they fix all their scythes upon long poles, and being very scarce of ammunition (though they had guns enough), they resolve to sally forth out of both their castles, and to make a resolute assault upon the enemy's camp on a frosty night; which they did perform with such irresistible courage and good success that they made such foul work and havoc amongst their enemies that such persons as were not cut in pieces or mangled with these terrible weapons were either taken prisoners or forced to run away, and leave their camp as it was. This valiant exploit and prosperous adventure frighted the rebels so much (though they were ten to one) that they never offered to besiege them any more till the 15th of June following, all the country being entirely theirs, saving these two small holds."*

Among the prisoners were some leaders of the rebels, in exchange for whom the Bishop and his sons and Mr. Clogy were liberated. Bedell retired to the house of a minister named O'Sheridan, where he spent the short remainder of his apostolic life peaceably, and died after

* Clogy, pp. 214-15.

a short illness, on the 7th of February, 1642. He had desired that his remains should be interred beside his wife's in the graveyard of Kilmore Cathedral, which was now in possession of the Roman Catholic Bishop, to whom application had to be made to permit the burial as desired. This prelate, who is represented by Mr. Clogy as a sot, at first refused to permit the burial of a heretic in his consecrated ground, but at length was persuaded to give his consent.

"Minister Sheridan and I," says Mr. Clogy, "went to Kilmore about my Lord's burial, to speak with the Popish usurper, Bishop Swiney (as his name is so is he), who said to us at first:—' The churchyard was no more to be defiled with heretics' bodies.' Thus did these barbarous, ungrateful miscreants requite this servant of the Lord evil for good, who sought their welfare, and did them more good (even to the hazard of his own quiet and reputation) than all that were ever before him in that see. They would scarce allow him a place to lay his head on when he was alive, and now they will hardly allow a place for his dead body to lie, as right officers of that great city, which is spiritually called Sodom and Egypt, where our Lord is daily crucified. . . . So on the 9th day of February, 1642, he was laid in his grave—according to his desire in his last will and testament, hard by his wife's coffin that had been buried there four years before. The chief of the Irish rebels accompanied the corpse from Mr. Sheridan's house to the churchyard of Kilmore in a great solemnity, and desired Alexander Clogy, the minister of Cavan, to perform the office for the dead (according to our manner in former times), and promised not to interrupt in the least; but we being surrounded with armed men, esteemed it more prudent to bury him as all the patriarchs, prophets, Christ, and his Apostles, and all saints and martyrs in former ages were, than to attempt such office (and sacrifice for the dead, as they call it), and needless at such a time in the presence of those Egyptians. But instead thereof they gave a volley of shot, and said with a loud voice, '*Requiescat in pace, ultimus Anglorum!*' For they had told him at their first rising that he should be the last Englishman that should be put out of Ireland, because he was stiled by men of understanding, '*Ultimus et Optimus Episcoporum.*' "\*

They thus paid this mark of honour to this excellent man, the only one they knew how to offer, and such as they would have paid at the obsequies of their own chief. The Bishop's family remained at Mr. Sheridan's house till June the 15th, 1642. Immediately before this date, the Scots who held the two castles of which we have spoken, came to terms with the insurgents, stipulating that they should march out with some arms and all their movable goods that they could carry away with them by horse or cart towards Dublin.

"So on the 15th of June, 1642, in the eighth month after the rebellion, we marched away, above 1,200 men, women, and children, after they had eaten the cows' hides which had covered their cabins and huts from Christmas till June. A sad company of poor people we were, as ever was seen together; some loaden with children on their backs, many with two little ones in their arms, yet all rejoicing in the Lord for our enlargement at last. About 2,000 rebels accompanied us for our lifeguard, according to the articles of our agreement which were written by Archdeacon Price, but now Archbishop of Cashel. The Scots had about 300 horse, some of them well appointed, for our guard also, under the conduct of Sir

\* Clogy, pp. 229-31.

Francis Hamilton and Sir Arthur Forbes. Major Bayley had his foot company of Scots that lay at Cavan, and had made their escape in the night to those two castles, with all their arms, and the train-band with them. The country had orders to bring provision for money, which they did in great plenty."*

They set out on the 15th of June, and reached Drogheda on the 22nd. Sir Henry Tichbourne, governor of Drogheda, met and took them under his protection, with a party of horse and foot, ten miles from Drogheda. Their march was very leisurely, if they were in dread of being murdered by the Irish through whose districts they had to pass. On the 15th of June they marched seven miles; the 18th, four miles; the 19th, three miles; rested on the 20th; the 21st, six miles; and on the 22nd they met Sir Henry Tichbourne.

"The rebels that conducted us," says Mr. Clogy, "took solemn leave of us, being sore afraid at the sight of our English forces; they hasted away, having kept us seven nights in the open fields, without anything over or under us, but what each of us had about us; yet they offered us no violence, save in the night when our men were weary with continual watchings they would steal away a good horse and run off, but were very civil to us all the way, and many of them wept at our parting from them that had lived so long and peaceably amongst them, as if we had been one people with them."†

I submit these statements of the Rev. Mr. Clogy, a

* Clogy, pp. 241-2.   † Ib., p. 243.

man prejudiced even savagely against Irish Roman Catholics, respecting what he witnessed with his own eyes, without comment, that the reader may form his own opinion as to how far they are, or are not, in accordance with his introductory denunciations, and with Sir John Temple's History. Mr. Clogy concludes as follows :—

"Most of our poor pillaged company came towards Dublin, a poor exhausted city of refuge, which was neither able to lodge us, nor to relieve us with things necessary, thousands dying every week, being pierced through for want of the fruits of the earth, as is at large set forth in the book of Dr. Jones, dean of Kilmore, who wrote the history of the horrid rebellion; as also by Sir John Temple, a worthy and honourable privy councillor, before and after that calamity."

I repeat that I hold England and Scotland guilty of every death that took place under these circumstances by "want of the fruits of the earth," after the fugitives entered the walls of Dublin.

I have already admitted that, considering the position of Sir John Temple as Master of the Rolls and Privy Councillor, and his residence in Ireland during the civil war in Ireland, from 1641 to 1652, nothing short of the most stringent evidence contradictory of his statements could justify our rejection of them. Such contradictory evidence, however, studiously taken, to avoid cavil, from Protestant authorities, has been set forth in the preceding narrative. I think it advisable to refresh the reader's memory by summarising it as follows :—

1. The statements of Lords Justices Parsons and Borlase, laid before the Long Parliament on the 1st December, 1641, and Temple's letter to Charles I., dated 12th December, 1641, describing horrible murders and atrocities then perpetrated by the Ulster insurgents, are proved to be absolutely false by the proclamation of the same Lords Justices, dated 23rd December, 1641—the precise time, two months after the outbreak, when, according to Sir John Temple, the whole Protestant population of Ulster had been cut off.

2. Archbishop Laud, in a letter to Strafford, dated July, 1638, states that he had been informed that the Ulster Protestants were able at that time to produce 40,000 fighting men. Major Morgan, Member of Parliament for the County of Wicklow, makes exactly the same statement in a speech in the House of Commons; and Lord Clarendon himself states that in 1648 "the Scots in Ulster were very numerous and possessed considerable towns." No pretence of a second plantation of Ulster, either before or since then, has ever been advanced.

3. The war was vigorously prosecuted for some months in Ulster with nearly uniform defeat of the Roman Catholics, and with extreme excess of loss of life on their part. Their exceptional victory of the Laney was due to the Highland dirk and broadsword.

In less than eight months from the commencement of the war their leaders admit that they are completely vanquished, and debate the necessity of at once abandoning the struggle and expatriating themselves to seek better fortune abroad. This defeat was accomplished by the Ulster Protestants absolutely unaided, and, alone, amounts to a demonstration that Temple's statement does not remotely approach to truth.

4. If that statement were near the truth, Ulster ought to be by far the least Protestant province of Ireland. It has ever been, however, since James's plantation, and is now, by far the most Protestant.

5. The preposterous discrepancies as to the amount of murder and massacre, from 300,000 to 5,000 lives, throw discredit on the testimony of each witness.*

6. While Cromwell's courts-martial condemned to death 200 individuals in the other three provinces, in which no general massacre of Protestants was ever alleged, in Ulster, where a massacre throwing into the shade the Sicilian Vespers and the massacre of St. Bartholomew was perpetrated, one man, Sir Phelim O'Neill, was found guilty and executed.

## IX.

My most earnest and anxious desire and hope is that a *real* and affectionate union between Great Britain

* See Appendix.

and Ireland may be accomplished; not the false union of 1801, brought about notoriously by the most scandalous bribery and corruption, equally disgraceful to the bribers and the bribed; and which has been for seventy-eight years justly regarded, by an immense majority of the Irish people, as one of their worst wrongs. A true union between the two countries is the common interest of both. I am confident this will be slowly but certainly secured by the dogged perseverance on the part of England in the complete reversal of her policy in the government of Ireland, adopted since 1829—unmoved by the brainless and contemptible yet provoking tactics of each crop of trading Irish patriots. Indeed I am satisfied much progress has been already made towards this consummation.

My parting counsel to my dear Celtic brethren is this:—"Let Erin remember the days of old," but with the special object to contrast the oppressions of old with the benefits conferred upon her by the old oppressor since 1829. They are too numerous to be specified here. I will mention three or four of them.

(1) The Irish National Education, perfectly free from any just suspicion of tampering with the religious belief of any sect—offering an excellent education, availed of at present, more or less completely, by upwards of 1,000,000 of children, and supported by a parliamentary grant of £651,091. Contrast with

this the system supported by Parliament from 1747 to about 1825—the Charter Schools, of which there was one for each county. About 1,400 children were lodged, fed, clothed, and educated in these schools, on condition that they should be brought up Protestants. In 1784 the truly great and excellent Howard visited Ireland for the purpose of enquiring into the condition of the prisons. He chanced to inspect some of these schools, and was so shocked by what he witnessed that he used his influence to procure a parliamentary inquiry into their management. The committee appointed to inquire reported that—

"The children were sickly, pale, and such miserable objects that they were a disgrace to all society; that their reading had been neglected for the purpose of making them work for their masters; that they were in general filthy and ill-clothed, without shifts or shirts, and in such a situation as it was indecent to look on; the diet was insufficient for their support; and in general they had the itch, and other eruptive disorders."

The grant, they said accordingly, was expended—

"For the purpose of imprisoning, starving, beating, diseasing, destroying the natural affections, and letting the understanding run to waste of 1,400 poor children annually, under the pretence of instructing and converting the young generation."

(2) The Encumbered Estates Act, by which the ruined Irish landlords were swept off and replaced by successors who possessed at least the ability to do their duty by their estates and tenants.

to vapour in the theatre of Ireland, the very girls will hoot him off the stage.

But let us suppose the impossible achieved, and that Ireland has shaken herself free from all connection with Great Britain. How wretched would her condition be! She would be at the mercy of any petty naval power on the Atlantic seaboard which might take umbrage at any of her proceedings. The Ultramontanes would, at least at first, carry everything before them, and a crusade would forthwith be declared to re-instate the Pope in his rightful possessions. A fleet of merchant vessels would be equipped, carrying ten or twenty thousand men, to accomplish this pious purpose. They would be met, of course, outside the Strait of Gibraltar by a squadron of iron-clads and gun-boats despatched by the King of Italy, which would speedily (in spite of a predicted shower of paving-stones on the sacrilegious Italians) send them to the bottom of the Atlantic; and, if his Majesty were minded to give a never-to-be-forgotten lesson, his fleet would be ordered to proceed to Ireland, with directions to bombard our sea-ports, burn every ship, vessel, yacht, and boat round the Green Isle, and to declare a blockade of all our ports, so as to preclude our taking a herring or importing a pound of Indian meal, of tea, or sugar, or cotton, or flaxseed, or tobacco. Denmark, Holland, Belgium, or Portugal could without difficulty inflict the same miseries upon us in case of quarrel.

The alternative offered us (of which, indeed, we are now in possession) is that we should form no unimportant part of the most powerful empire in the world, with security against bombardment or blockade, and with the blessings flowing from the full and fair participation in the wisest, the most stable, and the freest constitution the world has ever known. This is a bird you have in the hand. How many of those in the Home-Rule bush is it worth?

I deprecate everything that tends to keep up ill blood between Great Britain and Ireland, and therefore, before I lay down my pen, I beg leave to petition all writers, newspaper editors, and others, who have to deal with Irish affairs, or follies, or unreasonableness, to deny themselves the mischievous and malicious pleasure of the biting sneer or gibe with which they so frequently season their Irish articles. These are, in the words of " the philosophic historian whose writings will instruct and delight the last generations of mankind,"* the "*Facetiæ asperæ quæ acrem sui memoriam linquunt.*"†

    * Gibbon.      † Tacitus.

(3) The Poor-law, before the enactment of which the destitute were mainly supported by the poor. Now the landlord, who contributed little, and the absentee, who seldom contributed at all, are obliged to contribute in proportion to their means.

(4) The Parliamentary Grant for the relief of the sufferers by the Famine of 1846-7, to an amount exceeding what in the world's history was ever bestowed in a similar calamity by any nation for the relief of its own starving people.

(5) The Act for the Reform of the Irish Municipal Corporations. These corporations had been strongholds of Orange or high Tory Protestant ascendancy till now. Roman Catholics had, indeed, been made eligible to them during the English scare occasioned by the revolutionary proceedings in France ; but for forty-seven years after not one Roman Catholic had been elected to the Dublin Corporation. Now they are not only eligible but elected everywhere.

(6) The Act for the Disestablishment and Disendowment of the Established Church of Ireland—worth, with reference to the pacification of Ireland, more than all the rest.

You are too sharp-witted, my dear fellow-countrymen, not to know that the last will-o'-the-wisp lighted for you by the Home-Rulers is a fraud. You know as well as I do that nine out of ten of these patriots care not at all for Home-Rule but as a means of attaining to separation from Great Britain, which is at the bottom of their hearts. Such separation, you are quite aware, could only be effected by force, and where is the force to effect it? You do not yet know the force you would have to overcome to compel the separation, but your children will know it. The British Empire has about a sixth part of the land-surface of the whole earth, and nearly a fifth of the population of the world under her dominion, not to mention that "Britannia rules the waves." Within the last fifty years the population of England has doubled—Ireland's, within the same time, has fallen off above two millions. Her present population is not twice that of London alone. A few years ago the United Kingdom crushed a rebellion, at a distance of several thousand miles, of 50,000 well disciplined and well armed infantry, horse, and artillery; and two absurdly called Irish rebellions, one in a cabbage-garden, the other at a few police-stations, with a handful of Constabulary. England cannot and certainly will not ever permit the noble Cork harbour to be converted into a Franco-Irish or Yanko-Irish naval station, with a Sebastabolic fortress at its entrance.

The result of the Irish National Education will before very long make every young Irish peasant, nay every young Irish woman, acquainted with these and other such facts; and then, alas for the gasconade of the trading Irish sham patriot! or, if he ventures still

185

APPENDIX.

*Note to page* 178.

THE following estimates have been made by Protestant writers respecting the numbers of Protestants murdered in the Ulster Massacre of 1641. May makes the number slain in the first month of the insurrection, 200,000. Temple, 150,000 in the first two months, or 300,000 in two years. Rapin gives 150,000 in about four months; the Long Parliament, 154,000. Lord Clarendon says 40,000 or 50,000 were murdered before the Protestants suspected any danger. Hume adopts this estimate. 37,000 perished within the first year according to Sir W. Petty's computation, which Carte adopts. The Rev. Dr. Warner asserts that in the two first years of the Rebellion 12,000 Protestants were slain; of whom, however, only 4,000 were murdered. Cooke Taylor, a Protestant of a Cromwellian family, says:—"After a very careful examination of all the statements, the present writer believes that the number of persons killed by the insurgents was less than 5,000; and that about an equal number was slain by their opponents."* Now, with such preposterous discordance among the witnesses, what is the testimony of any individual witness worth, unless he fully and clearly sets before the reader the grounds on which he builds the conclusion at which he has arrived?—which not one of them does.

There are two historians who have in latter times given narratives of this sad period, for one of whom I entertain profound respect, and for the other much respect. The former, Lord Woodhouselee, in his admirable epitome of Universal History, says:—"Ireland, during these transactions,

* *Civil Wars of Ireland*, vol. i., p. 264.

exhibited a scene of horror and bloodshed. The Irish Roman Catholics had judged these turbulent times a fit season for asserting the independency of their country, and shaking off the English yoke. From a detestable abuse of the two best of motives, *religion and liberty*, they were incited to one of the most horrible attempts recorded in the annals of history. They conspired to assassinate, in one day, all the Protestants in Ireland, and the design was hardly surmised in England till above 40,000 had been put to the sword."* The latter, Mr. Green, in his excellent *Short History of the English People*, 1875, p. 524, says :—" A conspiracy, organised with wonderful power and secrecy, burst forth in Ulster, where the confiscation of the settlement had never been forgiven, and spread like wildfire over the centre and west of the island. Dublin was saved by a mere chance ; but in the open country the work of murder went on unchecked. 50,000 English perished in a few days, and rumour doubled and trebled the number. Tales of horror and outrage, such as maddened our own England when they reached us from Cawnpore, came day after day over the Irish Channel. Soon depositions told how husbands were cut to pieces in the presence of their wives, their children's brains dashed out before their faces, their daughters brutally violated and driven out naked to perish frozen in the woods."

Lord Woodhouselee, I am persuaded, relies upon the authority of Hume; and Mr. Green, I suspect, accepts the relation of the same historian, whose own thrilling narrative (suggestive of " quills upon the fretful porcupine "), in his eloquent, beautiful, and pure English, is based mainly on Temple's romance; although he himself throws strong discredit on the veracity of the Irish historian. " By some computations," says Hume, " those who perished by all these cruelties are supposed to be 150,000 or 200,000. By the most moderate, and probably most reasonable account, they are made to amount to 40,000; if this estimate itself be not,

* *Universal History*, vol. vi., p. 125.

as is usual in such cases, very much exaggerated."* Let us give the great historian all the credit and "honour due" for having thus humanely spared the lives of at least 120,000 of his fellow-creatures.

Temple, in his History of the Rebellion, gives what he calls sworn evidence of about 100 murders. The testimony in full half of these cases is to the following effect :—" I, *A. B.*, swear that I was told by *C. D.*, that *E. F.* murdered *G. H.*"† The oath is good no doubt as to the fact of *A. B.* having been told this by *C. D.*; but has no bearing whatever on the truth of *C. D.'s* report, and is therefore quite irrelevant. Mr. Webb, in a recent valuable contribution to Irish history, says in his article on Sir John Temple :—" A careful collation of the evidence of these eighty deponents shows that but fourteen of them testify to what they saw themselves. (The evidence of the others is entirely hearsay.)"‡

\* Hume, vol. vi., p. 442. Dublin : 1780.
† Temple's *Irish Rebellion*, pp. 84-124. London : 1812.
‡ *Compendium of Irish Biography*, Alfred Webb, p. 520.

www.ingramcontent.com/pod-product-compliance
Lightning Source LLC
Chambersburg PA
CBHW032134160426
43197CB00008B/644